Planning for London   Penguin Special

Judy Hillman, now planning correspondent of the
Guardian, has been writing about the changing face
of London for eight years. Sussex-born, she was
educated in Canada and at Brighton, Hove High and
Roedean schools. She then went to St Andrew's
University to take a degree in economics and moral
philosophy. She has also been a planning
correspondent of the London *Evening Standard*
and the *Observer*.

Planning for
London

Edited by Judy Hillman

 Penguin Books

Penguin Books Ltd, Harmondsworth,
Middlesex, England
Penguin Books Inc., 7110 Ambassador Road,
Baltimore, Maryland 21207, U.S.A.
Penguin Books Australia Ltd, Ringwood,
Victoria, Australia

First published 1971
Copyright © Penguin Books Ltd, 1971

Made and printed in Great Britain
by Hazell Watson & Viney Ltd
Aylesbury, Bucks
Set in Linotype Plantin

Contents

London Quotes

'When a man is tired of London he is tired of life; for there is in London all that life can afford.' – Dr Johnson

'Some people live in houses and they don't bother to paint them. I will like if, you know, London was cut up into little villages and long roads between them.' – Seven-year-old boy, 1970

'I think they have got too many houses all stuck together. They look very dull. I am happy that the heath does not make it all jumbled up like a rabbit hole. It's not houses, houses, houses. There's at least a place where children can play. I would like London to be something like the New Forest. It's a bit too crowded, I think. Supposing you were hovering up in an aircraft, you would see how busy and dreadful London is.' – Boy almost nine, 1970

'I don't actually have enough love for London at all to think in terms of if only that was done then I would like it better. I dislike the crowds and the fact you can never see for any great distance. Probably I would most like to see the slums go, then the new garish egg-and-chip shops with the great fluorescent For Sale notices. The most important thing is to make London cheap enough for a natural society to live in.' – Computer programmer, 1970

'The Westway is marvellous. There should be a fast road to the south coast. It's so difficult to get out of London.' – Married woman, 1970

'Everyone commutes. None of one's work colleagues live in London. London's going the same way as New York – the very rich or the very poor or the single.' – Financial executive, 1970

'Unfortunately today too many people are leaving London not because they are tired of life but because they are tired of London.' – Mr Peter Boydell, QC, at the opening of the inquiry into the Greater London Development Plan, 6 October 1970

Introduction

There are times when the planning of a great city like London can seem ineffectual. The beautifiers and the bureacratic believers in tidy urban utopia have endlessly tried, for example, to transform Piccadilly Circus, at present a tawdry but magnetic crossroads for traffic and people. However, nothing has happened – except a succession of plans and photogenic models. Elsewhere, the city's experts dreamt up bright new car-free shopping streets and precincts. During the years of preparation those areas began to die and by the time the builders moved in trade had vanished and the clinical expensive units took years to let. Meanwhile new areas have broken through to fame and fortune without the help of any official vision or encouragement. The King's Road has progressively changed from a normal neighbourhood street into golden acres for trend-setting fashion and expensive antiques. Portobello Road and Camden Passage have become Saturday hunting grounds for junk and antiques, Carnaby Street a Mecca for visitors. Yet none of these was planned.

Of course, such happenings are small scale in relation to the whole panorama of the London scene. But even on the grander scale the planners have all too often failed to get the urban picture quite right. For years the experts were worried about London's rising population and aimed to hold the numbers at the eight million mark by decanting overspill (that dreadful word) into the new and expanding towns outside. Yet in the meantime, the real problems were changing. Immigration, particularly of unskilled workers from the Commonwealth, was concealing the basic downward population trend; the increasing loss of middle-income families who could only afford the life they wanted beyond the green belt; the growing polarization in London itself, where economic and social pressures create ever larger areas of concentrated prosperity near the centre; the twilight housing with its miserable overcrowding and the massive municipal urban renewal which could too easily deteriorate into the city's future slums. To be fair, it was some of London's planners who spotted the changing pattern and London's politicians who, for a while, were slow to believe that the capital could all too easily follow on the unhappy trail laid out by New York and other American cities.

Now London again has a plan through which it is hoped to retain all that is good and improve the rest. But will the city really become a better place in which to live? Will more households have better homes that they can afford? Will car owners find it easier to drive and park? Will public transport become tolerable? Will there be sufficient staff to keep regular bus services on the road? Will there still be corner shops as well as supermarkets? Will jumbo hotels and mass tourism be absorbed into the city scene without wrecking traditional London?

It would be encouraging if even some of the answers were likely to be affirmative. But it seems much more likely that, once again, some things for some people will improve, with or without a push by officialdom, and some things for some people will deteriorate. New problems will arise, because man, the planner, even backed by computer and complicated city models, can never hope to have complete control.

If platitudes and expressed aims could provide answers to urban ills the future, as sketched by the Greater London Development Plan 1969, would be reasonable. But perhaps it was too much to expect the Greater London Council to produce a really honest assessment of the situation, emphasize all the known difficulties in clear unequivocal language, outline and cost possible options, select some, and then state the legal, financial, administrative and physical obstacles along the chosen route.

However, politicians are still politicians and few believe that an electorate is able to cope with intelligent discussion of the alternatives and difficulties ahead. So the picture was painted bright.

The GLC did and does have its local difficulties. First there was internal dissent with bitter power struggles and jealousies between rival departments, between the planners, the architects, the engineers, the research section. Reorganization has now taken place to combine planning and transportation, which may help in the long term but it came too late to affect the production of the plan. Then the engineers reigned supreme. They had all the facts and figures from the £1,250,000 traffic survey to prove their case for roads, though some of their projections have since gone astray. The planners, whose department got off to a later start in the newly created regional authority, were always fighting a rearguard action.

There was also the GLC's delicate relationship with the thirty-two boroughs and the City Corporation. In typical British tradition, the London Government Act of 1963 created thirty-three large principalities and divided planning responsibilities, except for the main highway network, between them and the GLC. For success, there would have had to be angelic cooperation. With normal dissident human beings involved this was asking the impossible. So the GLC could, for example, point out London's housing need, warn of impending crisis but feel unable to force the outer boroughs to come up with the necessary goods. For there to be any real progress, such suburban areas, where life is more spacious, clean and green, have to help out and absorb families from the congested, decaying centre. But to many, central London, its people, its difficulties, belong to another world. Why should they provide homes for families who they are convinced will need rent rebates, whose children will be ill behaved and probably vandals, who may well be coloured and so cause additional community problems? Such areas still hanker for the time when they were independent country towns, unaffected by creeping city growth.

And these problems arise constantly in other fields. The GLC would like to see a brighter Thames but is largely dependent on the riverside boroughs and the Port of London Authority for results. It can make very acceptable noises about recreation and development prospects of the canals but do little. Perhaps it was not so surprising that the consortium between the GLC and the two boroughs of Westminster and Camden for the redevelopment of Covent Garden was dissolved because the senior authority thought it would be too cumbersome and slow.

New York can let pedestrians take over Fifth Avenue on summer Saturdays, but London still gives the car free rein in some of the greatest shopping streets in the world – partly because GLC engineers consider that the role of the road is to ease the traffic flow, but partly because so many consultations and essential agreements are necessary before any progress can be made. Even Carnaby Street, which was an obvious and simple candidate, has taken years. The same pattern of obstacles hinders, too, the more general introduction of environmental areas with through traffic forced out of its habitual short-cuts and back onto the main road network.

With so many organizational obstacles it sometimes seems miraculous that constructive ideas ever get off the ground. And this is particularly true if one considers the long complicated planning processes as originally ordained – a GLC strategy, a detailed inquiry, possibly modifications, perhaps another inquiry, borough strategies, borough inquiries and only then plans for action. This has, of course, now been simplified.

However, no city, let alone London, can remain static under the pressures for change. So the GLC is allowed a separate inquiry for its grand West Cross Route behind Earls Court, a motorway which, when built, will kill off the houseboat community of Chelsea and seal the Embankment's fate as a major through-road. The prospect of mass tourism, aided by temporary but generous government grants, has resulted in a rush to plant huge hotels, many of which will be checking in visitors before the next stage of London's planning is officially in hand. Southwark may play host to a modern version of Shakespeare's Globe Theatre, the Covent Garden Market area is bound to change once the wholesalers finally move to Battersea and the sight and smell of fruit, flowers and vegetables so near the heart of London will become a mere memory. The South Bank lands between Waterloo and Blackfriars bridges are in the process of transformation with the building of a National Theatre, headquarters for London Weekend Television, and the King's Reach development with its homes, offices and hotel. Even British Rail is at long last thinking positively about the potential of its acres at Waterloo Station. And the same pattern continues outside the centre as inner London terraces are converted into expensive leasehold flats for the young and rich, as shopping streets expand, as housing estates grow. The need for local strategies may now have been removed but the time-lag through the official procedure is still slow.

With these changes new problems will no doubt arise. It is too easy now to understand why the Isle of Dogs had its brief era of revolt. The land was cheap and council homes were built with little regard for its isolation and extremely poor communications with the East End and the rest of the city or for the lack of local cheap shopping of the sort newcomers would expect. To the long-standing resident, the Dogs is a very special place, with the tang of river life to offset its obvious inconvenience. To the family moving out of a slum clearance area on the mainland it has little to offer except a new home at a cheap rent.

At Thamesmead, where the GLC is building up a community for 60,000 people, the land was also cheap. Again the area is remote, the transport connections bad. It is too early to know how this development will turn out, whether private enterprise will be able to produce homes of satisfactory design (to justify the international award) at prices hundreds of families can and want to afford, or whether the final imprint will be one of a gigantic council housing estate.

This matters, because such large slabs of building have rarely matched up to the kind of community London's former villages provided in terms of income and social mix. There were mews for servants and coachmen behind the smart houses of Belgravia until the rich took them over for their own use. Till recently, the now chi-chi cottages of Chelsea and Fulham did house people who were by no means rich. The East End did have its professional enclaves. And the cottages of Hampstead Garden Suburb were originally built for workmen.

But the emerging new London rarely provides for different kinds of people to live within range. For the areas of private ownership, paint and prosperity, this may not be serious. But social decay, even the growth of ghetto living, could all too easily set in elsewhere. By 1974, it is expected that 76 per cent of the homes in Tower Hamlets will be council owned. The figure for Barking is 69 per cent, 60 per cent for Southwark, 57 per cent for Hackney, 41 per cent for Lambeth and Islington. Already individual estates have their problems. Others, high-density schemes with tower blocks or mass-produced deck access slabs, would attract few tenants by choice. What will their future be, as go-getting households, prodded into action by rising rents, try to buy homes of their own, in all probability outside London altogether? Can they avoid becoming the slums in the 1970s and 1980s? Would a more flexible letting policy to allow all comers, people on larger incomes, the young flat sharers, help? It certainly will not be as easy to pull down or bulldoze some of the monumental blocks as it was to erase four-storey brick terraces. But how is the city to ease the plight of the poor and/or deprived? The GLC shrugs this off as fundamentally a matter for central government, but buck-passing up or down the bureaucratic hierarchy is no answer.

Cities all over the world are faced with the same problems as London – how to improve life in the slums, how at the very least to provide educational and other opportunities for the children who grow up there, how to come to terms with the car, how to provide adequate public transport, how to retain essential comforting character in the face of pressures which create international anonymity, how to find the cash to keep the city serviced.

This Penguin Special tries to discuss some of these aspects of life and planning in London. There are obvious omissions, in particular any detailed consideration of the hundreds of communities that nestle inside the built-up mass and for most people are the London they know. It had been hoped the GLC might allow one of its recent publications, in condensed form, to appear as a general scene-setter. However, finally, this form of public participation did not appeal. So instead of the proposed official contribution, David Wilcox has distilled some of the main themes. The rest of the contributors, who include three academics, three journalists, three architects and a planner, differ widely in their outlooks, indeed would sometimes wish to push or pull the city in opposite directions. But they do share one important thing in common – they care about the future of London.

Judy Hillman
1.11.70

The Greater London
Development Plan   David Wilcox

Most Londoners expected a plan for the future of their city to
tell them whether the disused factory site over the road would
be a new council estate, how the roads would be unjammed or
noisy lorries kept out of their street, and when Piccadilly Circus
would be rebuilt. Perhaps, with a few airy ideas about mono-
rails thrown in, some forceful worthy promises about clearing
the slums, improving the bus services and making life more
tolerable with decent shops and somewhere for the children to
play.

It would have been a triumph – and a surprise – if the Greater
London Council could have put forward its Development Plan
in March 1969 and met with universal public acclaim and excitement. It just was not that sort of plan. Flipping through the
seventy-seven-page *Statement*, or even looking at the two enormous nine-section maps, it really seems rather a thin document
to describe how London could change by 1981.

It says a lot of people are leaving town for a better house in
the country. It estimates that a lot of houses are in terrible condition, but does not say much about what can be done about
them, or how families can afford to stay in London. There is a
bit about office floorspace, but that does not say which workers
London needs most – clerks or civil servants, waiters or factory
hands.

The residents of Croydon, Ealing Broadway, Ilford, Kingston,
Lewisham and Wood Green are told they should get massive
shopping centres to serve the surrounding areas, and one chapter
says Londoners need more parks, but not exactly who will get
them or how. We will also, the GLC says, be more careful not to
let developers ruin the skyline with tower blocks in the wrong
places, and we will protect historic buildings and attractive areas
so long as the pressures to redevelop are not too strong.

An appendix sets out 'areas of opportunity' like the docks, where massive undefined changes are likely as trade moves down to Tilbury, and 'action areas' which include old town centres, Victorian slums, disused airfields and marshes due for major redevelopment.

And then there is the chapter on transport. This puts forward the Greater London Council's road plan – three new motorways circling through London, with the Ministry of Transport building a fourth in the Green Belt. New radial links replace the old trunk roads with motorways to take traffic in and out of London, and there will be some improvement of the present 'secondary' roads. The cost started out around £860 million and is increasing. At least 20,000 homes will be demolished over the twenty- or thirty-year programme.

The roads plan proposed by the GLC was the one element the householder could relate to his neighbourhood. If a motorway demolished his house he would get compensation. Perhaps worse, if it passed near by he would get none. And there were and are plenty of prophets of doom to forecast how motorway traffic would flood the quiet residential streets as it joined and left the new primary road system. Inevitably the plan has been identified with the motorway programme. So the result of the GLC's initial presentation was often uproar at public meetings with officers and councillors. Everyone wanted to talk about the roads, and were not interested in the rest of the plan. After all, there was not much in it, was there?

Action groups were formed along the line of the ringways, coordinated by the London Motorway Action Group under the chairmanship of Douglas Jay, Labour MP for Battersea North and former President of the Board of Trade. Ringway-bashing became a favourite public sport of the militant middle class during 1969 and 1970, with the GLC accused by its opponents of concealing evidence of the disastrous impact the new motorways would have on the environment, their rising costs and the Los Angeles-type situation they might bring.

All this was rather less than fair to the GLC. They had produced a rather poor plan, perhaps, but that wasn't entirely their fault. The plan is the first attempt in Britain to produce a 'structure plan'. Instead of setting out in detail the future use of land – the precise location of new homes, schools, major and minor roads, factories, parks and so on – the aim is to produce a flexible framework for the 620 square miles of Greater London, while recognizing that many of the pressures for change are outside the council's control.

The strategy plan should indicate how many people will live in London, how there will be enough jobs for them, and how they will be able to travel to work, fetch the kids from school, go out for a meal, or visit relations on the other side of town.

The details of local planning are to be carried out later by the thirty-two borough councils and the City of London. The Greater London Development Plan roughs out the grand design, but the boroughs will do the detailed drawing. At present it is not clear how the details will be formulated, because in the middle of the inquiry into the GLDP the Government announced its intention of abolishing borough structure plans. Unfortunately, in practice, this has led to a situation in which the GLC promises much, but cannot say how or when all of it will come about. Except, that is, for the motorways. Because the GLC is the executive body these have a fairly well defined timetable and often quite precise routes.

The broad aims of the plan, set out in Section 2 of the *Statement*, are vague enough to be unexceptional: 'It is the council's intention,' says the first paragraph, 'to do everything within its power to maintain London's position as the capital of the nation and one of the world's great cities.' This will be done by fostering industrial and commercial prosperity, and cultural status, particularly for those activities which operate best in London. The living conditions of Londoners will depend on this flourishing prosperity.

On the broad issue of how many people do, and should, live in London, the plan recognized a marked change in thinking. For thirty years planners had been trying to restrain the growth of London by the choker of the Green Belt, and to ship people out of their overcrowded homes in inner London to new jobs and better homes in the new towns like Harlow and Stevenage, Bracknell and Crawley. By the mid 1960s it was clear the battle was won. In 1939, there were 8,600,000 Londoners, by 1961 it was 8 million and by 1969 about 7,700,000. The GLC strategy planners calculated it could fall to 7 million by 1981 – a figure they later revised down still further to about 6,800,000.

The reason for the fall is partly lower birth rates, but particularly because large numbers of young families have left the city to find better homes on the other side of the Green Belt. They are voting with their feet against living conditions in London, even if they then have to commute.

There are advantages in that the falling population reduces the enormous pressure on housing. But the disadvantages, argued the GLC, is that London could end up short of 700,000 workers. At least, this was argued in 1969; the tone has changed since. So conditions should be improved to try to hold the population between 7,100,000 and 7,300,000 and balance the work force with reasonable housing conditions.

The other great challenge to the good life in London is the impact of motor traffic and 'The council sees no way of avoiding, over a period of years, a massive programme for the improvement of the road system'. Hence the ringways, aimed to keep London moving and allow traffic to be diverted out of the congested residential streets on to the motorways. At the same time the broad aims of the plan are to conserve 'the features which give London its distinctive character', improve the standards of design of buildings, and keep the Green Belt.

It is a little difficult to define the plan exactly, because several volumes are involved. The statutory document is the written *Statement*, together with two maps. But the analysis line of GLC thinking must also make use of the *Report of Studies*, which contains much detailed exposition and research findings, together with some ideas from the GLC publication *Tomorrow's London*. More detail on transportation studies is contained in *Movement in London*, and further information became available with evidence given in the public inquiry into the plan which opened on 6 October 1970.

Housing and population

Driving out of London, it is fairly easy to trace its growth, like the rings within a tree. First the surviving houses of the great estates in central London – Georgian terraces and squares, some still expensive homes, some converted offices: Bedford, Portland, Portman ...

Then the inner ring of Victorian suburbs, built for well-to-do merchants as the railway made short-distance commuting easy, particularly in the north and west. And to the east small two-storey cottages for London's working class. By 1914 the urban area extended 5 miles from the centre, roughly corresponding to the old London County Council area.

After 1918 electrification and extension of the railways created the new suburbs, engulfing the old town and village centres. These inter-war houses are less tightly packed, often detached or semi-detached, and stretched twelve to fifteen miles out until development was halted after 1945 by the Green Belt.

London's housing problems correspond, to some extent, to this historical growth. Many of the solid Victorian homes are no longer occupied by professional people, but are split up into bedsitters and flats, often overcrowded, with shared bathrooms, lavatories and kitchens. The outsides may be dirty, the gardens overgrown, the roads full of litter and the shops scruffy – twilight areas where no one feels it is worth spending money on property.

The small nineteenth-century East End houses – often jerry-built – present different problems. Although there may be less overcrowding, the structure of the houses is often unsound, and they lack bathrooms and lavatories.

In the inner boroughs a great deal of the private property is rented, while in the spacious outer boroughs most is owner-occupied.

Broadly, the GLC believes that the way to tackle London's housing problem is to move some people out of London altogether, and to move some from the overcrowded inner boroughs to new homes built in the outer boroughs. About 80,000–90,000 more people leave London each year than come in. There are

50,000 more births than deaths, so the net fall in population is about 40,000 a year. About half of this is to 'planned overspill' schemes like the new and expanded towns.

At first sight this loss of population should help solve the problem of not enough decent homes – even though it may lead to an increase in commuting. The snag is that although the population has fallen by 1,300,000 between 1951 and 1966, the number of households increased from 2,619,000 to 2,690,000 because people are leaving home to get married younger, are better off, and live longer. So, if everyone is to have their own home, the demand is increasing.

The other snag about the falling population is that those who move out tend to be the young skilled families with prospects. Retired people are living longer, and the average age of London's working population is falling. If present trends continue the GLC estimated in the Plan that there could be a shortage of 700,000 workers in London by 1981 – and an inflationary wage situation which could lead to still more commuting.

And as the number of households increases the demand for small flats and bedsitters increased, particularly near central London, to provide homes for young couples, office workers and students – a demand which is obvious to anyone hunting through the classified ads and accommodation agencies.

The GLC wants to improve housing conditions for Londoners. The *Statement* says:

> The council's overriding aim, in collaboration with the borough councils, will be to secure a progressive improvement in the environment so that London as a whole becomes a much more attractive place to live in than it is at present; a place which offers better opportunities for its children and young people to develop, which meets better their needs for physical and mental recreation.

Mr Bernard Collins, the GLC's joint Director of Planning and Transportation, put it more strongly when giving evidence to the public inquiry: 'Improvement of housing is the most vital step in improving the whole environment of London life.'

The aims are there, with a fairly extensive definition of the problem. There is not, however, much in the plan about how they are going to be achieved. The boroughs, not the GLC, will have to build most of the new homes.

The extent of London's housing problem is set out in the *Report of Studies* – a dry chapter of statistics behind which can be read an appalling situation in which one Londoner in ten is badly housed. A survey carried out in 1966–7 for the GLC using a 4 per cent sample showed that by 1981 216,000 homes would become structurally obsolete unless action were taken – 9 per cent of the total of homes. The same would be true of another 347,000 in the next ten years. Eleven per cent of homes were found to have no bath, 11 per cent to have no lavatory, and 7 per cent to have neither.

It is very difficult to convey in statistical terms just how over-crowded many Londoners are, and how bad their homes, though it is obvious there is severe overcrowding in some areas, that a large number of houses are not fit to live in, and even more are decaying fast. The survey showed a crude shortage of 273,000 dwellings in London – 273,000 families and people who want to live alone but who cannot get a place of their own. The figure does not take any account of whether the place is decent enough to be called a home – or whether it is a near slum without hot water, a bath or inside lavatory.

The housing problem is concentrated, as might be expected, in the older inner boroughs. Tower Hamlets, Newham, South-wark, Lambeth and Hackney, in particular, have thousands of houses without modern amenities. Overcrowding is worst in north Kensington, north Westminster and Islington.

The situation is made more desperate in these housing problem areas because they lack the other essentials of decent life in the city. The schools are often grim barracks, designed in the last century to contain the attention of children by high windows and no distractions. Outside school there are no parks in which to play – only streets made dirtier by factories, workshops, gar-ages and scrap yards scattered among the houses. About one million Londoners live in these 'stress' areas. Nearly half the families share accommodation, a quarter lack a bath, and a quar-ter an inside lavatory.

The *Statement* says little about how these problem areas should be tackled – although the *Report of Studies* is a little more helpful. It suggests broadly that the old jerry-built cottages of the East End should be demolished to make way for new homes, while the sounder, but overcrowded, houses in the north and west could more often be converted and rehabilitated.

It is clear that most of the new housing in the older areas will have to be provided by the local authorities. In 1966 and 1967, 81 per cent of the building there was done by councils. The *Statement*, however, says:

The council's policy throughout London is that private enterprise and housing associations should be encouraged to assist the efforts of the public housing authorities. This will increase the choice and variety of housing, give some relief to public financing and help to create balanced communities.

There are no housing-target figures in the *Statement*, although there is a table of population estimates which has been strongly contested by some boroughs which feel they are expected to lose too many people. Just how many houses are needed depends on the population – and the number of people staying in London depends on how good the housing is.

A better idea of the state of London's housing emerges from a report published in the summer of 1970 by a joint study group of Ministry of Housing and local authority officers. *London's Housing Needs in 1974* assesses the shortage of 'satisfactory' homes in London at any time, which includes both the crude shortage due to overcrowding and the need to improve several hundred thousand homes lacking basic amenities.

The report concludes that in mid 1969 there was a crude deficiency of 233,000 homes, which roughly tallies with the GLC figure. It predicts that in 1974 the deficiency will be 106,000. More important, perhaps, it estimates the shortage of satisfactory homes in 1969 as 553,000, falling to 336,000 by 1974. This fall will only come about if private builders continue to put up 10,000 homes a year while local authorities increase their output from about 21,000 a year to 32,000. Most of the deficit will be in inner London.

The GLC, since the plan was published, has announced its housing programme up to 1981. Taking the numerical shortage of 273,000 homes in 1967, the GLC estimates that in the 14 years to 1981 some 262,000 homes will be demolished, of which 192,000 come down because they are unfit and 70,000 to make way for new roads, schools and other works.

Another 100,000 homes are needed as an operating float – some must always be empty as people move to new homes, and some are second flats and houses for people living out of town. This adds up to 635,000 homes needed between 1967 and 1981.

The supply is to be made up of 330,000 built by local authorities, 150,000 by private builders and housing societies, and another 60,000 gained by converting large old properties. A supply total of 540,000. This gives an admitted shortage of 95,000 homes in 1981 – which is a crude shortage not counting the thousands of unsatisfactory homes.

The evidence given by GLC strategic planners at the public inquiry was not encouraging. The message was that although the shortage of houses is being reduced, the condition overall of houses is deteriorating.

The GLC still believes that the fall in population should not go completely unchecked, but stresses more than ever before that the price and condition of housing are the crucial factors in keeping families in London.

Some critics of the GLC plan suggest that a population of between eight and nine million is desirable. The GLC replies that they should aim for only that size of population which can be decently housed. And with the present state of available accommodation and the shortage of land, these higher target figures are impossible.

The experts also warn that most of the new building will have to be done by local councils unless special grants are made to private builders to make their participation worth while. Even so, families generally are likely to have to spend more of their income on housing in future. Their daunting assessment was that 'about half the one person households would need to spend about a third or more of their incomes even if they rented sub-sidized public housing. This is without including rates.'

The GLC has found itself in the position of stressing housing as the single most important factor in improving the quality of life in London – but being unable or unwilling to take the steps to tackle the problem. It cannot force the outer boroughs to take families from inner London and build them homes, it has not the resources to do the job itself, and it cannot rely on private enter-prise. Housing ordinary middle-income people in London just isn't good business.

Employment

London may have a lot of brolly and bowler commuters, well-paid executives and civil servants, but it also still has a great number of factory workers. And the capital could not keep going without the thousands of basic service workers like postmen and dustmen, sewage workers and bus drivers. With the increase in tourism, hotels need large numbers of cleaners, waiters and kit-chen staff.

Quite a few mothers go out to work – and, until 1961, there were twice as many people living and working in London as dependants, like school children and retired people. But since then large numbers of young middle-income families have moved out, and by 1981 the ratio will only be one and a half to one. The result, says the GLC, will be that economically the workers will have a greater burden to bear – through paying rates – in providing education and welfare services.

Other trends include the gradual switch from manufacturing to clerical work, and the fact that London tends to have more well-paid workers and more poorly-paid than elsewhere.

Not only is London losing the middle-income workers, but the total work force has been falling since 1966, so that by 1981 there could be many more jobs than workers.

Some of the people who have left London for a better home may be expected to continue to work in town – getting a cheaper, better home but spending more on commuting. So far this has only happened to a limited extent. In 1966 there were 470,000 daily commuters into London, a figure which is expected to increase to between 510,000 and 540,000 by 1971. By 1981 it may be 550,000 – not enough to balance the number of people moving out to jobs somewhere else. The number travelling out of London each day is expected to be 100,000 in 1981 – the same as 1961.

The GLC is worried about this loss of workers because it could lead to an inflationary situation with some firms facing constant labour shortages, and jobs being done by people not quite up to the tasks – leading to losses of efficiency. Increased commuting is not the answer partly because it would be so expensive to make improvements in the railway system to carry more passengers at peak hours.

This problem of a work force which is getting smaller in numbers and on average older, polarized between the rich and poor, has forced the GLC into considering just what and who London really needs.

It was fashionable in the early 1960s' property booms to react against glass and concrete office towers because of the extra congestion they would bring to the centre. When the Labour Government came into power in 1964, George Brown imposed severe restrictions on new offices. The Location of Offices Bureau has struggled manfully to persuade firms to move out. But the GLC argues that an answer to the labour shortage will not be found by trying to move offices out – and even suggests some small increase in office space beyond the mid 1960s' allocations. Easing of Government restrictions now means that planning permissions from the GLC, rather than office development permits, set the limit.

Factories are a different matter, particularly where they are in residential areas. The sites could be bought up for housing, the firms moved out, perhaps to a new town, and everyone would gain. Provided, that is, the moves out are not so rapid that local unemployment is created, as happened recently in some areas of south-east London.

To justify more office development the GLC stresses that it is important to keep up the level of the capital's economic activity. Firms pay rates, good wages and even finance development themselves to renew the city's fabric. (Although higher wages are certainly needed – in 1969 22 per cent of London families had an income of less than £20 a week.) Instead of trying to ship out entirely this source of wealth, London should be more choosy about which firms are allowed sites in the city, giving preference to those firms which demonstrably need to be there. Obvious examples are the insurance, banking and finance operations of the City, which contribute so much to the country's balance of payments by their invisible exports. These firms will stay – and there is a case for allowing the greater office space that modern organization demands. On the other hand, a domestic motor insurance firm could be expected to do just as well in the suburbs or out of London altogether.

How the GLC can select the right businesses for London is not fully worked out. And even if planning permission for new offices were only given to the chosen firms, it might still be difficult to prevent them from letting to someone else.

Greater economic activity would bring higher wages which in turn would mean that more families could afford better homes, spend more generally – and pay higher public transport fares so reducing public subsidies.

There is little in the plan about the poor, except to say that they will live in council homes, paying fair rents and getting rebates if necessary. The ultimate solution of their plight lies with the Government, says the GLC.

Of far greater concern is the trend for the middle classes to quit the sinking city ship because they cannot afford to buy a decent home with a garden for their children. In 1967, 85 per cent of Londoners couldn't afford a mortgage on a £5,000 home – and with prices rocketing, there are few around in that range.

The GLC's analysis of employment does not make clear how shift workers in central London – such as waiters or postmen – will be able to afford to live near their work and avoid struggling with an expensive and inadequate public transport system at odd hours.

There are indications that the GLC will soon have to look more carefully at the lower-paid end of the wage scale. One obvious example has been the tremendous growth of hotel development in central London and the growth of tourism will demand still more beds. The GLC will have to consider whether to encourage an industry which depends on a low-paid labour supply. Where will the waiters and cleaners find homes?

A more domestic example was provided on the day the public inquiry into the Development Plan opened. As the lawyers carried their briefs into County Hall, striking sewage workers employed by the GLC picketed the doors demanding higher wages with which to support their families in the increasingly expensive capital.

Transport

Two conflicting trends dominate any attempt to plan London's transport system. People want to move around more, so they are buying cars. Secondly these cars are making life increasingly intolerable with their noise, fumes and appetite for road space.

The GLC put forward the motorway plan for London as the means of tackling both ends of the problem. The new roads, up to eight lanes wide and sometimes constructed on concrete stilts like massive flyovers, are to provide the road capacity to get London moving. They will also allow traffic to be diverted from the residential streets increasingly suffering as drivers look for ways to avoid the jams.

However, such motorways are extremely costly – over £10 million a mile in some places – knock down large numbers of houses, and divide communities. Apart from these obvious draw-backs, distinguished critics have prophesied that the roads will merely encourage more traffic and cause as many problems as they solve for surrounding streets. They argue for alternatives to the motor car instead of consecrating a costly and very permanent memorial to the most destructive influence on our cities.

The GLC, however, forecasts economic doom if the roads are not built. The *Statement* warns:

About twice as many households are expected to own cars in 1981 as in 1962. If the present road congestion is allowed to develop London's efficiency will be so impaired that not only will its businesses suffer but so also will its vital services such as fire and ambulance, refuse disposal, and the distribution of food and goods. The higher costs and lower levels of service which would result would lead to more people leaving London. This is already happening.

The main reason for the congestion, says the plan, is that most of the roads are radial, carrying vehicles in and out of town, while more and more people want to travel across and around London. This is not always easy. So the GLC will build a new primary network of motorways, but it will be up to the borough councils to designate 'environmental areas' between the roads where through traffic should be excluded from residential streets.

The primary network consists of three ringways, and some new radial roads, like the spokes of a wheel, joining the hub of the ringways.

Ringway 1 – also known as the 'motorway box' because of its shape – is planned to supplement the old nineteenth-century road system of the areas around Central London. In the north it runs from Willesden to Hackney Marshes, and in the south from Clapham Junction to Kidbrooke. The west side runs down through Shepherds Bush to Chelsea Creek, and across the river. In the east the route is from Hackney Marshes through the Blackwall tunnel south of the river.

This ringway is perhaps the most controversial, although it is not planned for completion until the 1990s. The east cross route is already being built, and the southern approach to the Blackwall tunnel is open. The west cross route is planned for the early 1970s. It has, however, provoked vehement opposition from the people of Chelsea because the bridge over the Thames may not follow immediately and traffic will then flood along the already congested Embankment. The north and south cross routes are not scheduled for completion until the 1990s, but they are being hotly opposed because they carve through some of the most densely populated areas of London and demolish, for example, some fine Victorian villas at Belsize Park and Blackheath.

Ringway 2 consists basically of two sections. The northern arc includes the present North Circular widened by the Ministry of Transport, and improved to avoid hold-ups from traffic lights or crossing traffic. The southern arc takes the form of a new motorway running from Chiswick and Barnes through Wandsworth, Norbury and Eltham to Falconwood and crossing the river near the new town of Thamesmead.

Ringway 3 passes through the outer suburbs, circling London 12 miles from the centre, and is intended to provide for traffic, which would otherwise penetrate much deeper into the built-up area.

Outside London the Ministry of Transport will build what is in effect Ringway 4, known as the North and South Orbital roads.

The radial system planned includes the new M11 and M23, and extensions to the M1 and M4. The A1, A2, A10, A13, A20, A3 and A40 are all to be improved 'to high capacity standard'.

In the *Statement*, the GLC argues that 'Ringway 1 provides an opportunity to improve an unsatisfactory environment. Much of its route lies through obsolete areas which urgently need rebuilding.' Enclosing an area with a population of 1,500,000, it should, according to the GLC, help reduce traffic penetrating central London.

Local pressure from people living along the lines of the ringways has forced the GLC to reveal a good deal of detail about routes, design and likely noise levels. The secondary road system has been given less attention, although the policy of continuing to use these main roads in future for heavy traffic may be equally important for as many people.

Although Ringway 1 is designed to take some traffic which would otherwise fight its way through the heart of London, it will do little to reduce central congestion. Oxford Street and the Embankment, Edgware Road and Trafalgar Square will be just as busy and probably worse. Westminster City Council, responsible for two thirds of the central area, has argued that more money should be devoted to secondary road improvements, including tunnels under Hyde Park, and a tunnel underpass in front of the Houses of Parliament to relieve Parliament Square. But the GLC is unmoved.

In his evidence to the inquiry, Mr Bernard Collins, the GLC's chief planner, said: 'The problem of travel outside central London is the crucial one for this plan.' He stressed that nearly all Londoners live outside the centre, and most work outside as well, and 'there should be little discernible difference between the life style of outer London and that of the Regions.' He added that the benefits of car ownership would also be valuable in the more cramped conditions of inner London: 'Public transport can offer a reliable basic service but there are circumstances when it is not a satisfactory or realistic substitute for a car for most people of the kind envisaged as forming the future population of London.'

Behind Mr Collins's words stands the worry that the valued middle-class high-wage earners will only stay in London if they can own and use a car.

Even so, this sizeable roads plan is linked with a policy for restricting car use through parking controls, particularly in central London. An area of forty square miles, controlled mainly by parking meters, is intended to force potential motorists on to public transport as far as possible. Stricter control of off-street parking will discourage the commuter.

The GLC's attitude to having public transport is in a state of flux, the council only having taken over London Transport at the beginning of 1970. There is no control, of course, over British Rail. The *Statement* says: 'The basic pattern of the rail system is well suited to London's needs and will continue to provide for the majority of personal journeys to central London, particularly the peak journey-to-work movements.'

Not much hope there of support from the GLC for massive investment to make life more tolerable for the commuter – although the need for some improvements is recognized. Where these are made will depend more on the success of British Rail's negotiations with the Treasury and the new Department of the Environment, than on anything the GLC may say.

The *Statement* says little of the underground system, although, since the plan was published, there has been evidence of much more support for extra tube lines and improvements. The GLC is backing the new Fleet line from Baker Street through central London to New Cross, and the Piccadilly line extension to Heathrow Airport. New trains have been ordered for the Northern line, and more will follow for other lines.

Nor is there much in the *Statement* on buses. They are recognized as continuing to provide the basic public transport for short trips, and the GLC is working on schemes to improve reliability, including bus priority lanes.

The proposals for development of strategic centres at Ealing and Wood Green, Ilford, Lewisham, Croydon and Kingston, to concentrate shopping, office development and community facilities will also be linked with public transport developments.

Townscape

Hardly a week passes without some threat to the character of London from large new projects. It may, for example, be a scheme for a hotel twice the size of the Hilton in a previously quiet residential area. The locals understandably feel outraged by a proposal for a massive block of 1000 bedrooms which will dominate their skyline and choke the roads with coaches bringing in jumbo-jet tourists.

Or perhaps it is a plan to build a car park under another London square, with possible damage to the trees above and unsightly ventilation shafts and exit ramps. Bloomsbury Square has followed Cadogan Place, Knightsbridge and Cavendish Square, behind Oxford Street, amid furious protests.

The greatest heat currently seems to be generated by the threat of demolition to any of London's 20,000 historic buildings. The Euston Arch and Carlton Mews have gone, but the Tate Gallery portico stays and the Government was forced into a public inquiry over Norman Shaw's Scotland Yard.

The GLC has some fairly tough planning powers to control the worst ravages of the face of London, set out in the section on town and landscape in the plan. Historic buildings will be preserved 'in all proper cases'. In addition, borough councils should designate conservation areas where new development must at least be in character with the old. In this way, the old village and town centres like Richmond and Greenwich, Harrow-on-the-Hill and Enfield, should retain their charm although surrounded by suburban sprawl. The London squares must be preserved, trees retained and more planted where possible. Open land within London including playing fields and golf courses, cemeteries and allotments should not be built on – and, of course, the Green Belt is to remain sacrosanct.

If the statement is rather sketchy on these important issues there is more detail in Chapter 8 of the *Report of Studies*. Here fascinating maps show the 137 great estates of central London – Portman and Bedford, Grosvenor and Cadogan – and areas of particular importance within inner London are listed. Some, like Belgravia and the smarter parts of Kensington, are in little danger. Their special character is protected against badly-designed new buildings and property values are so high that there is seldom lack of money to restore shaky structures. But in others, urgent action is needed to prevent attractive property, perhaps 100 years old, crumbling into a seedy jumble of over-crowded rooming houses, with buildings decaying beyond repair. Large areas north of the Bayswater Road, between expensive Holland Park and the slums of Notting Hill are like this. So are parts of Islington.

The *Report of Studies* sets out a programme of action for conservation areas including the need for tight controls on new buildings, historic building grants and traffic schemes to take cars and lorries out of residential streets. Unfortunately this is summed up in just two paragraphs in the *Statement*.

The apparently random spread of high buildings in London since the early 1950s – council flats and office blocks – has completely changed the roof-top panorama of many areas. Pedestrians are dwarfed by the new scale of city architecture. In the City, St Paul's and the Wren churches have lost their dominance to the skyscrapers, and the silhouette of the Houses of Parliament across the river is fudged by new government office blocks behind.

Developers now find it more difficult to get permission for towers that would destroy the character of an area. They will not be approved where they threaten famous views and long-distance vistas, from, for example, Primrose Hill, Greenwich Observatory and Telegraph Hill. High buildings are thought unsuitable around the royal parks – although the Royal Lancaster Hotel, the Hilton and Knightsbridge Barracks have already destroyed Hyde Park's rural illusion.

Nevertheless high buildings are not universally frowned on in the plan – and in some areas are encouraged. The tower blocks at Croydon give an exciting definition to the town centre. The Millbank tower is an interesting element on the Thames scene, without challenging the Houses of Parliament. Permission may be given for towers where a pattern of high buildings has already emerged – along Edgware Road, and in some parts of the City.

Some of the plan's most detailed local proposals emerge in a section on areas of metropolitan importance or areas of special character, future action and opportunity. These read like a tourist itinerary – Whitehall, the Tower of London, the South Kensington museums, Bloomsbury, the City and so on. Their historic buildings and vital functions give London its unique character, and planning policies should aim at safeguarding this. The *Statement* gives a brief run-down on the major aims for each area:

Care should be taken of the views and skylines around Whitehall, and through traffic removed as far as possible between St James's Park and the Thames. Within areas of the City, buildings should be preserved and ancient street patterns retained. In Bloomsbury, preservation should be tempered with recognition of the needs of the university.

Of course the real test only comes when a scheme challenges one of the ideals, but is presented as a practical necessity. For example, the university may want to demolish a Georgian square to provide better accommodation for its cramped departments. The previous Government wanted to demolish Scotland Yard to make way for new offices. The GLC has itself proposed a road through the middle of historic Greenwich.

Action areas form the second category of metropolitan importance – areas where either local authorities or private enterprise may be expected to carry out major schemes within the next ten years. They include suburban town centres like Barking and Bromley, Orpington, Enfield and Harrow, Surbiton, Mitcham and Wimbledon. Within the ring of Victorian suburbs around central London action is proposed to renew old high street areas like Brixton, Lewisham, Peckham and Hammersmith Broadway.

In central London, King's Cross and Victoria could be redeveloped as more efficient transport interchanges – although the first depends on a decision about London's third airport, and the second has been set back by official preference for extending the underground to Heathrow instead of the proposed British Rail link.

Camden Town, London Bridge and – hopefully – Piccadilly Circus are included, as well as the massive scheme to redevelop and rehabilitate the Covent Garden area when the Market moves to its new site at Nine Elms, Battersea, by 1973.

Some of the most exciting potential is in the East End, where hundreds of acres are ripe for change as dock trade moves down to Tilbury. St Katharine Dock is to be a prestige mixed development of export centre, hotel, marina, entertainment centre and housing. London Docks will provide new homes for council tenants, and the East India and Surrey Docks also offer redevelopment potential.

The issues are vital to the character of London, but their resolution will depend on day-to-day political priorities rather than the acceptance or rejection of the plan.

London in the Region   Derek Senior

'The strategic policy for the distribution of population and employment in South East England is at present under review in a government-sponsored joint study. Matters could emerge from this review which would react upon and necessitate changes to the Plan, possibly even to the general employment policy.'

So said the authors of the Greater London Development Plan in the introduction to their *Statement*; and how right they were. Matters have emerged in the report of the South East Joint Planning Team (since published under the title *Strategic Plan for the South East*) which do indeed necessitate quite radical changes in the plan, and especially in its general employment policy. So far as inner London in particular is concerned, they necessitate a complete reversal of that policy.

Inner London, in this context, means the old LCC area minus Greenwich plus Newham and Haringey, but excludes central London – the area within the elliptical ring of main-line railway termini. On employment in central London, the Greater London Development Plan (GLDP) and the Strategic Plan for the South East (SPSE) are at one. As the latter puts it,

the role of central London as a national and international centre for administration, finance, commerce and tourism is of considerable importance to the national economy, and consequently an objective of the regional plan should be to provide scope for the expansion of this specialized role.

Endorsing this view, the GLDP rightly observes that to give the activities essential to central London more opportunity to develop does not necessarily mean giving them more space, for the proposed development of a hierarchy of shopping and office centres in outer London will enable central London to become more selective – to concentrate on the more highly specialized services which cannot economically be provided elsewhere. But it does mean allowing a marginal increase in the floorspace available for these more specialized facilities (including administrative offices) and making it easier for the providers and users of their services to travel in and out of central London. All this is not in dispute.

What is in dispute is whether such control as planning authorities have over the distribution of population and employment should be used to encourage, or to restrain, the spontaneous outflow of manufacturing industries and their skilled and semi-skilled workers from London (and especially from inner London) to new or expanding towns and cities beyond the Green Belt. On this the policies put forward in the GLDP and the SPSE are diametrically opposed.

The Greater London Council is bent on retaining those kinds of manufacturing industry – engineering, vehicles, electrical goods and the like – which are unrelated to the essential functions of central London, and which readily move to new and expanding towns precisely because they can operate more profitably there than in congested inner London. Accordingly it seeks to reduce the rate at which their labour supply is dwindling in London – an aim which it can itself pursue only by promoting the greatest possible increase in London's housing capacity, in the hope that this will retard the accelerating voluntary dispersal of its population, and by effectually ceasing to cooperate in the planned movement of Londoners and their jobs to new and expanding towns. At the same time it demands a 'strict control' over 'the creation of new opportunities for employment in the outer metropolitan region beyond the built-up area of London', combined with a relaxation of the present control (by means of industrial development certificates) over the building of new factories within London. It even calls for a reconsideration of the 'implications' of the Industrial Selection Scheme (which puts employers in new towns in touch with appropriately skilled Londoners who want to live and work there) on the ground that it is 'depriving London of some of the types of labour which are particularly scarce'.

The South East Joint Planning Team, by contrast, concludes that 'an objective of the regional plan should be to stimulate, as appropriate, the mobility of employment within the region and to encourage in particular the further dispersal from London of employment in both manufacturing and service industries which can be located satisfactorily elsewhere'. It goes on to say that increased specialization of employment at the centre, coupled with the need to improve living conditions, community facilities and the environment generally for those who necessarily live in or near the centre, means that those activities which are not essential to the specialized role of Greater London must be reduced. These considerations, it adds, reinforce the need for further decentralization of manufacturing industry and some office employment.

This flat contradiction does not arise from any incompatibility of basic premises: indeed the Joint Planning Team went so far as to adopt the GLC's unwarrantably optimistic assumption that its area's population would not shrink to less than 7.3 million by 1981 if enough houseroom could be provided for that number within it at acceptable occupancy rates. It arises quite simply from the fact that whereas the Joint Planning Team was looking at the South East as a whole, and seeking the distribution of employment that would enable the region to make the most productive use of its resources, match employment with population growth and solve its major social problems, the GLC was concerned only with the 'economy' of Greater London, and particularly with the costs and benefits of alternative employment and population policies to its own corporate 'economy' – delicately referred to in the GLDP Statement as that 'on which Londoners rely for improving the environment'.

Tomorrow's London – a Background to the Greater London Development Plan dealt more forthrightly with the 'distinct role in our economy' of the technologically advanced industries that have supplied the bulk of the movement to the new towns. 'They contribute to our rateable values', it said; whereas some of the traditional consumer-goods industries, employing less skilled labour, 'contribute more to traffic chaos, to problems of waste disposal and to the lowering of neighbourhood amenities than they do to rates'.

This is not to denigrate the GLC or the authors of its plan.

They are democratically accountable only to the ratepayers of Greater London, and they calculate that by 1983 the implementation of the GLDP will be costing those ratepayers up to an extra 2s. 6d. in the pound in debt charges alone, even if they do succeed in retaining inner London's industrial hereditaments. They did not draw the boundary that confines their jurisdiction and concern to the built-up core of that indivisible planning entity, the London Metropolitan Region. But attention must be drawn to the consequences of that political decision in order to make it clear that the Minister, advised by the South East Joint Planning Team, now finds himself in the same position vis-à-vis the GLC as the GLC described itself, in *Tomorrow's London*, as occupying vis-à-vis the Greater London boroughs:

In this situation we cannot merely say to the Boroughs: put forward your structure plans, and we will tell you whether you can do what you want to do within your areas, or whether you must modify your proposals. Rather, we have to say: these are the constraints, this is the strategy which we regard as necessary in the light of the movements which we have measured and the trends which we see at work. Today it has become impracticable for any one London Borough, on its own, to plan its population or its employment without reference to the total housing and land situation. . . . If we propose populations in some inner Boroughs below the figure which they themselves had hoped for, it is not to diminish their stature, but to enable them to create an acceptable environment for people of all kinds.

'An acceptable environment' – that is the crux: the need, as the SPSE puts it, 'to improve living conditions, community facilities and the environment generally for those who necessarily live in or near the centre'. Who are the people who *necessarily* live in or near the centre'. Not the 'top brass' of central London's essential service industries, who can live where they choose; not the middle-echelon professional workers, who can afford to commute from the outer suburbs; and especially not the skilled and semi-skilled employees of manufacturing industries that have no need to be in London at all. They are the army of comparatively low-paid, unskilled service workers – the clerks and cleaners, the stage-hands and shop assistants, the waiters and porters – without whom, as *Tomorrow's London* testifies, the metropolis cannot function. These people have no choice but to live in inner London – the zone within five or six miles of central London which dates from before the First World War and contains all of the 'housing problem areas' identified in the GLDP, including the 'areas of housing stress' where some 300,000 households share 111,000 dwellings, most of them built at 'seriously excessive densities' and now in bad structural condition. They are poor people, and getting poorer, not because they get lower wages than skilled manual workers in Lanarkshire, Durham or north-east Lancashire – they don't – but because they have to pay about five times as much in rent for similar accommodation.

The reason why these intolerable conditions persist in inner London is obvious enough. It is that the service workers who necessarily live there have to compete for living space with the extensive premises and half a million operatives and clerical employees of manufacturing firms that could work more cheaply and efficiently in less cramped and congested locations. It is this intense competition for space that inflates the price of land to £150,000 an acre and more, drives up the rents of shoddy shared houses to an impoverishing level, and makes it prohibitively expensive either to replace slums with decent dwellings at tolerable densities or to create an acceptable residential environment.

Seven inner London boroughs have less than two acres of publicly accessible open space per thousand people – one of them less than a third of an acre. The GLC proposes that this ration should be raised to four acres per thousand, with a 'first objective' of two and a half acres – exactly what the LCC proposed in its development plan of twenty years ago. But it despairs of attaining even this grossly inadequate standard by 1981 in the 'housing stress' areas, where the deficiency is greatest, because of their 'high land costs and heavy re-housing liability'.

The physical and social consequences of this pressure on space in inner London represent the region's biggest planning problem. It is a problem that would gradually solve itself, if the

GLC and the borough councils concerned would only let it; for people have been moving out of London, in order (as the GLC acknowledges) 'to gain more space and amenity in relation to their cost', at a *net* rate of more than 80,000 a year for the past decade, and at a proportionately higher rate from inner London than from any of the other five sectors into which the GLC divides its area for planning purposes. Over the same period employment in manufacturing industry in central and inner London has declined at an accelerating rate from about three-quarters of a million to about half a million, while service employment has increased.

These are strong trends, and if only the GLC would positively reinforce them the problem could be solved quite soon. But it is still a big problem: the inner London sector still contains nearly two fifths of all Greater London's industrial floorspace – nearly four square miles of it – and has by far the highest concentration of skilled manual workers, both male and female. And yet, instead of encouraging the further dispersal of inner London's skilled and semi-skilled industrial workers and a further reduction of its manufacturing floorspace, the GLC proposes to do all it can to restrain the one and reverse the other. Because the manufacturing industry is there, it argues, the prospective shortage of skilled labour must be averted; at the same time, because unemployment among inner London's skilled workers is high (by London standards), inner London's industrial floorspace must be increased. And because a planning authority has no more direct means of influencing the size of the skilled labour force, the GLC proposes to try to slow down the rate at which Londoners generally are moving out in search of more living space. How? By increasing London's residential capacity – at the necessary cost of reducing the average Londoner's living space.

It is, of course, true that not all of the industries in central and inner London that are officially classed as manufacturing can be satisfactorily located elsewhere. For example, that part of the 'paper, printing, publishing' category which is represented by the production of national daily newspapers is clearly one of central London's essential service activities, while some of the 'manufacturing' employment in the clothing and food-processing trades is directly ancillary to central London's *haute couture* and tourist services. The industries that can be most readily and satisfactorily located elsewhere are such manufactures as engineering and vehicle building, which between them accounted for half the outward movement in the first half of the last decade; yet it is precisely these industries that the GLC is most anxious to retain. Their departure, together with their employees and the equally dispersible routine clerical sections of many service undertakings, would make room, physically and financially, for a dramatic and otherwise wholly unattainable improvement in the housing and environmental standards of the humbler grades of service workers, so essential to central London's specialized functions, who necessarily live in inner London.

It is also true, of course, that not all of London's dispersible manufacturing and service employments can move far; but neither is it necessary, in order to create an acceptable environment in inner London, that they should. Very comprehensive researches into the post-war movements of sizeable manufacturing units in the South East were carried out by Economic Consultants Ltd for the South East Joint Planning Team. They showed that, while nearly half of the units contacted had relocated themselves since 1945, most of them had moved less than twenty miles – and the shorter their move, the higher the proportion of their less skilled employees they took with them. There is clearly a great deal of scope for a 'relay' system of dispersal, from inner London to outer London, from outer London to the outer metropolitan area, from the nearer to the further parts of the outer metropolitan area and from it to new and expanding towns and cities in other parts of the South East. But from the GLC's point of view only the first leg of this relay would be acceptable – and it cannot be run unless industrial premises in outer London are vacated. From the point of view of the region as a whole, however, as well as from that of the service workers who must necessarily live in inner London, it is essential that such a system be comprehensively planned and organized.

The GLC attempts to justify the retention of those manufacturing and service employments which it cannot pretend are necessary to central London's essential functions, or themselves need to be near central London, by claiming that in London they are more productive, in terms of net output per unit of labour, than they would be elsewhere – even though they might find it more profitable (as many have) to operate elsewhere. The evidence it adduces, though admittedly inconclusive, does indeed suggest that some of these dispersible industries (but not engineering, by far the largest) do better by this criterion south east of a line from the Solent to the Wash than in the rest of the United Kingdom, and better in the new London and South-East Standard Region than in the rest of the South East. But it affords no warrant whatever for the inference that the inner London units of such industries do better there than they would in agglomerations of similar scale on London's outer fringe, in large centres developed beyond the Green Belt, or in more distant new or expanded cities (like Peterborough) which already have a strong nucleus of engineering and vehicle-building industries. As the SPSE tersely puts it, 'The benefits which stem from large concentrations of industry are not confined to London'.

The SPSE also says:

The work of Economic Consultants for the team seems to indicate that, provided a few basic requirements are fulfilled, and in particular a suitable labour force is available, most firms can operate in a number of different locations in the region without jeopardizing their operational efficiency . . . linkages of various types (to suppliers and markets for example) are not so important within the South East as has often been suggested . . . there would seem to be little difficulty in attracting firms to most parts of the South, provided that the areas in question are attractive to staff and it can be demonstrated to employers that suitable labour will be available.

In other words, nothing but the hostility of the GLC to the planned movement of skilled and semi-skilled workers from inner London to big urban centres in and beyond the outer metropolitan area now stands in the way of a planning policy for the region that would serve four essential purposes at once:

to maximize the productivity of the South East's labour resources; to enable the skilled and semi-skilled employees of inner London's manufacturing and routine service industries to live and work in a healthy, agreeable and uncongested environment; to provide employment (which only big centres can provide) for inner London's surplus of unskilled workers; and to give the service workers who must live close to central London enough elbow room to enjoy adequate living space and civilized surroundings at a cost they can afford.

It is possible to find in the GLDP *Statement* and *Report of Studies* odd sentences, or parts of sentences, which if quoted out of context would suggest that the GLC still accepts the policy of decentralization to new and expanded towns; but in every case its lip-service to this policy is coupled with an implicit assumption or explicit qualification which in fact negates its ostensible adherence to that policy. In the same way, every statement it makes about expanding London's housing stock is coupled with one about raising housing and environmental standards which purports to qualify it but which, in the absence of any proposal to reduce the space pre-empted by industrial or other uses, in effect contradicts it. A prime example of this misleading doubletalk is the following:

> But with higher space standards being demanded by the community as a whole, action to increase the housing stock would be the most direct means of retarding the fall of population. [para. 10.21]

The only policy suggestion that would tend to reconcile the conflict between the GLC's professed objectives is that there should be 'a gradual redistribution of population following development' within Greater London, so that excessive densities in the congested inner sector can be reduced at the cost of raising densities in outer London. But even this exception is rendered nugatory by the GLC's failure to discharge its mandatory duty under Regulation 11(c) to include in its development plan a statement of general policy on residential densities. It has, in fact, expressly abdicated its responsibility for density control to the individual boroughs, being itself content to offer them cooperation in studying 'the possibility of providing good residential environments at higher densities than are customary', together with advice which is either emptily platitudinous ('It is important that the residential densities they allow shall be conducive to the highest standards of environment'), tautologous ('In normal situations density zones should provide for lower densities than those of the maximum density zone') or meaningless ('The total residential capacity planned within each London Borough should be at least within the population range shown in Table 1, page 17').

What is meant by 'at least within' may perhaps be judged from the fact that in presenting the population range referred to, the GLC expresses sympathy for the view of a number of London boroughs that its upper limit should be set higher, and invites them not to regard the upper figures as unalterable 'if their detailed studies prove that they are likely to have and to accommodate satisfactorily a greater population in 1981 than shown'. This, in effect, gives the inner boroughs *carte blanche*, and thereby offers the outer boroughs a valid pretext for withholding cooperation in the policy of internal redistribution. For it is common knowledge that it was the councils of the inner boroughs, where the present housing densities are most excessive, who forced the GLC to abandon its strategic responsibility for density control as the only alternative to having it openly flouted, and that their notions of what constitutes 'satisfactory accommodation' for housewives and young children are not shared by the National Society for the Prevention of Cruelty to Children. Left, as they now are, to their own devices in this matter, they will doubtless continue to pack their people into tower blocks.

Again it must be emphasized that this is not to blame either the borough councils concerned or the GLC, but only to expose the ineptness of the London Government Act, which conferred structural planning powers on both, requiring the boroughs to submit their development plans to the GLC only for comment *en passant* to the Minister, not for approval. It thereby obliged the GLC to defer to the boroughs on any issue which aroused strong feelings among any group of them, however ill-informed, unrealistic and incompatible with its own planning aims it knew their stand to be.

The inner London borough councils, democratically accountable as they are to their own electors and to nobody else, are not to be blamed for pursuing – and compelling the GLC to endorse – planning and housing policies which they believe will maximize their domestic and industrial rateable values, and thus minimize the burden on each individual householder of raising a given rate revenue. They can be blamed only for failing to realize that such policies defeat their own ends by raising to a much greater extent the cost of providing their residents with a given standard of housing, amenity and mobility; but no doubt they calculate that national subsidies and the rate equalization scheme will pass on enough of this extra cost to people to whom they are not accountable.

Neither is the GLC to be blamed if it accepts the limitations imposed by the London Government Act and accordingly makes the best bargain it can with the boroughs, eschews the policies it would surely have adopted if its area had comprehended the geographical scope of the metropolitan problems confronting it, and confines its attention to the sectional interests of the Metropolitan Region's continuously built-up core – the London which *Tomorrow's London* properly described as 'something of a fiction'. This is not the place to discuss the GLDP's transport proposals, except to say that Ringway 1 would clearly be less likely to get choked as soon as it is built if it did not have to accommodate the commuting and commercial traffic generated by inner London's dispersible manufacturing industries, and that to demand priority for both Ringways 2 and 3 over the orbital route linking the major growth centres of both outer London and the outer metropolitan area reflects a singularly myopic parochialism.

Given the London Government Act, it falls to the GLDP Inquiry Panel, in advising the Minister, to make good as best it can the lack of a plan-making authority for the London Metropolitan Region. Such an authority would be as much concerned to solve the region's most urgent and intractable social problem as to plan for the best use of its land and labour resources in the interests of the London-centred community as a whole. It would therefore recognize that, in the words of the SPSE,

If the pressure on land at the centre is not to increase, and the position of the less privileged is not to deteriorate, there is clearly a need to encourage or promote decentralization from inner London, so that redevelopment of obsolescent housing, modernization of community facilities and improvement of the environment generally in inner London may be undertaken.

It would also recognize the 'potential for short-distance movement from inner London of a number of semi-skilled and unskilled jobs'. And it would regard as a matter of complete indifference, not worth a moment's consideration, what might be the population left in the continuously built-up area now called Greater London when these movements had produced the desired result. It would base its plan, as the Panel should base its appraisal of the GLDP, on a fundamental truth therein enunciated only to be forgotten :

'To divorce London from its region would be false.'

Possibly the starkest single fact about the London housing situation is that there are not enough independent units of accommodation to go round. In 1966, when the last census was taken (and the census remains the most reliable guide to what is happening), there were roughly 2,400,000 'reasonably separate' dwellings in the metropolitan area and roughly 2,600,000 households who might be assumed to want separate accommodation: a crude shortfall of about 200,000 houses.

It only falls as low as this, too, if one makes two pretty indefensible assumptions. First, that a dwelling need not be completely self-contained to be a family home and, secondly, that 200,000 single young people and some elderly ones actually like living in shared accommodation. If one took the census figures at face value, the shortfall in 1966 would have stood at about 350,000 houses.

Some allowance has to be made, in any case, for mobility and for the second homes that are inevitable in a capital city. Between them, these added about 125,000 houses more to the 1966 shortfall. So by the most modest measure that can be considered acceptable, London in that year had a dwellings gap, as the jargon puts it, of at least 325,000 houses.

In human terms, this meant over 600,000 London families – a quarter of all the family-type households in the area – sharing their accommodation with other people. There have been changes since the census (more, in fact, in this area than any other), but the gap is still enormous. Today, there are still almost certainly about 500,000 London families in shared accommodation.

One may choose to see this as a problem of too many people, and it is undeniably true that one of the factors contributing to the ever better balance of housing and households in recent years has been the fall in population. But this should not be exaggerated.

The total loss means a very much smaller fall in the number of households. At current rates, it takes a 5 per cent loss of population to reduce households by 1 per cent, because the households that leave are larger than those replacing them. The reduction in household numbers has also been far less important than the increase in the number of dwelling units available.

It is a moot point, in any case, whether London should be welcoming this loss of population in the form it takes. For while families with children leaving to find better housing elsewhere means improved living conditions for them and more space per head for those who remain, the fact that they are being largely replaced by young single people and young couples (liable to leave, in turn, when they have children of their own) has a very unbalancing effect upon the community structure. As long as there are other means of improving the housing situation, an exodus of people should not be regarded as anything but a very mixed blessing.

For immediate and long-range considerations alike, therefore, there is no point in seeing the problem as anything but one of too few units of accommodation. Granted, this is not quite the same as a housing shortage. The crucial element here is an absolute shortage of household space. Unless sharing is accompanied by overcrowding, there is always a prospect of obtaining more units, possibly enough units, from the existing stock of housing. But what it does mean, at the very least, is extensive deprivation on one of the counts that essentially characterizes a home – namely, decently private living arrangements.

In practice, sharing in London involves a good many other deprivations too. Half the households sharing accommodation in 1966 also had to share a bathroom: about a third had no access to a bath at all. One in eight even had to share a stove and sink. The scope for achieving enough units through conversion dwindles sharply when one considers all the additional bathrooms and kitchens that these figures point to.

In addition, close on 10 per cent of them were actually living in conditions of acute overcrowding – with two rooms or less, one of these often a kitchen, for every three people. Shared houses are, in fact, significantly more densely occupied than other houses. Across the board, every 100 rooms in London had sixty occupants in 1966: in multi-occupied houses, there were seventy-three.

This situation is compounded by the state that far too many of London's houses are in. Only about 20,000 houses may be unfit for habitation by a strictly technical definition, but this is so strict that even the public health inspectors who have to work with it have the grace to blush at what it excludes. The GLC accepts that about 9 per cent of the total stock (roughly 200,000 houses) is at the end of its useful life. These houses are so far gone structurally that it is not worth fitting them out with the bathrooms and internal sanitation that they lack. To this category the Standing Working Party on London Housing (a body on which the local authorities and the old Ministry of Housing – i.e. the new DOE – are jointly represented) would add about 140,000 more, also short on these amenities, also ready for replacement, but worth limited improvements until the programme gets round to them.

This makes a total of about 340,000 houses (15 per cent of the stock) which fail right now to meet the minimum acceptable standard. Beyond these lie about 200,000 more that are nearing the end of their century and will be the next candidates for replacement unless repaired and modernized urgently. In all, a quarter of the stock is in an inadequate condition.

Since these poor housing conditions coincide extensively with shared accommodation for historic reasons, they add to the misery of dilapidation to living conditions already miserable for lack of privacy, comfort and space for many London families. They also diminish the advantage of privacy for many more.

From an operational point of view, however, they are a catastrophic handicap wherever they occur. For where they coincide with the unit deficiency they undermine the prospect of coping through a policy of conversion: where they don't, they add a pressing replacement problem.

Between them, in fact, the shortage of units and the inadequacy of existing units mean for Londoners a deficiency of decent housing half as large again as the total stock of housing in Birmingham, the nation's second city. At this moment, according to the Standing Working Party, London could use about 550,000 extra houses.

Before a figure like this – and the fact that London is now an almost totally built-up area – it's small wonder that eyes should be cast longingly at the Green Belt. Still, it's probably just as well that the Green Belt is untouchable. For it by no means follows that the acquisition of more building land would make any difference to the deficiency situation. Like out-migration, it would mean better conditions for individual families. It might, in fact, divert much of the movement away from London to the outskirts instead. But it would still leave the in-migration situation wide open. If, at the same time, it left the same houses standing within the existing built-up area that are standing there today – available on the same terms as at present – chances are that they would continue to be used in the same way.

There can, in fact, be no enduring solution to wretched living conditions unless the houses in which they are found are either altered or replaced. Until then, they will simply fill up again each time a family moves to something better. At best, they will be less densely occupied. It may be obvious why this is true of the houses in poor condition. To understand why it also applies to the houses that are being shared, one has to take a closer look at the relationship between houses and households generally.

Almost half London's houses are over fifty years old, in the inner areas up to 80 per cent. This accounts in large part for the shortage of amenities and extent of delapidation in such areas. It is significant, for example, that in the GLC's ring of 'housing problem' areas, surrounding the city centre, no less than 69 per cent of the houses were built, on average, before the end of the First World War. Even on the GLC's more modest definition of unsatisfactory housing, it found 45 per cent of London's total in these areas.

Where they are not already physically obsolete, however, old houses may be socially obsolete vis-à-vis the current population pattern. When one considers just how the population of London has changed over the past fifty years – one- and two-person households multiplying dramatically (increasingly of the young, but many elderly people among them), two-generation households dwindling both in numbers and size, three-generation households effectively disappearing and almost no one with servants now – it stands to reason that even the houses built for the tradespeople and bourgeoisie of fifty years ago will ill serve present requirements. Even the good standard housing of the interwar period in outer London (30 per cent of the stock) falls short against these changes, since it is overwhelmingly housing for the two-generation family in a London that has fewer of these with every year.

Right across the board, the distribution of London's houses by size is startlingly inappropriate. For a city with over half of its households consisting of one or two persons, it has only 10 per cent of its housing stock in one-, two- or even three-room dwelling units. At the other extreme, 20 per cent of the stock is in units of seven rooms or more (135,000 of them with nine rooms or more), while only about 6 per cent of households contain six or more people – and these, ironically, mostly to be found among the few households seriously overcrowded.

Since a large part of the stock is blocked off by small households with a very generous amount of space (a fifth of all the one- and two-person households, mostly elderly people in the outer area, have five or more rooms to themselves), the housing provision remaining is used as best it can by the remaining households. No less than a third of all London's households occupies that 20 per cent of the stock that has seven rooms or more. Each house with nine rooms or more contains on average three households.

In the older inner areas, where over half the houses with more than seven rooms and almost all those with more than nine rooms are concentrated, the 'fit' situation is, not surprisingly, worse than ever. In the housing problem areas, the GLC found that five households in ten, compared with about two in ten throughout London, were in shared accommodation.

Given the cost of maintaining a large unit in London, above all in the inner area, there is little prospect of these spacious houses going over to single-family occupation to any great extent. Even without the falling demand for large family accommodation in the inner area, the pressure for small family accommodation – and increasingly, for single-person accommodation too – gives their owners an incentive to keep them in use as lodging houses.

It is, therefore, just as vital on the sharing count as on quality that housing which no longer meets current needs in an acceptable manner should be changed, so that the problem should not perpetuate itself. The appropriate way of achieving change, however, is different on the two counts. The qualitative deficiency mainly concerns old housing that was never built to a decent standard in the first place, like the workingmen's warrens of the old East End. The unit deficiency, on the other hand, mainly affects housing built to a high standard in the same period – some of the worst deficiencies being found, in fact, in that built to the very highest standard. While replacement is going to be the main way in which the first can be tackled, the second should be remediable by way of structural alteration. Indeed, the scale of the first problem makes it essential that the second, wherever possible, should be so approached. It even makes it advisable, for pragmatic reasons, that much of the first should be tackled through the second-best solution of temporary improvement.

For replacement – though the most complete answer to squalid housing conditions (and, in theory at least, also the most flexible) – is crippled, as a means of achieving change, by the slow pace at which it moves. In 1969, only about 13,000 houses were demolished and only about 7,000 of these, because of other claims on the sites the others occupied, on grounds of unsatisfactory condition.

31,000 new houses were built, but it seems likely that about a third of these came from open sites – a source of land so rare in London now that they are known as 'windfalls' when they become available. Yet, despite this and the fact that at least two units were replaced for every one demolished (not to mention about 2,500 additional units provided through conversion), the total housing gain was of the order of 21,000 houses.

The pace of replacement can be accelerated. The last fifteen years have, in fact, seen an impressive increase in the rate at which new houses are added to the London stock: from a meagre 3·3 per 1,000 population in 1956, the annual figure is now up to 4·3. Still low beside the national average of 6·4 per 1,000, but quite high, by current standards, for a built-up area. Indeed, if all the building planned by the London authorities were to be carried out, without any falling off in the private building rate, by 1974 (according to the Standing Working Party) the figure could be six houses per 1,000 population – or 42,000 a year.

But this would still, in practice, amount to a gain of about 30,000 houses only, unless more units were to be provided through conversion. It would also leave well over 100,000 houses in the most unsatisfactory category and more than ever in poor condition beyond this because of galloping decay, unless improvement work also accelerated.

This is why the GLC has stressed the urgency of mobilizing other means of tackling the problems. But this could be advocated just as strongly from the planning point of view. For unless some of the pressures are lifted from the replacement programme, there is a danger that its key role of reshaping the pattern of life in the city – according to principles like community balance and devolution of activities – will be swamped by an unending series of straightforward slum clearance schemes. In the inner area, the opportunities provided by the need to replace are already being at best half utilized, because of the pressure to make the largest possible housing gain on every site.

Unfortunately, there are two fundamental obstacles to the success of this approach. The first is that the problem houses that so urgently need improvement and conversion are overwhelmingly in the hands of private landlords – and there is no sure way of persuading a private landlord to bestir himself. The powers of a local authority in this respect are almost completely lacking, by comparison with its power to act once the property becomes officially a slum.

There are generous incentives on hand, especially since the 1969 Housing Act. Half the cost of the work, including repairs which arguably should have been done years ago, can be charged to public funds. The other half, if need be, can be borrowed from the local authority at a rate of interest no landlord could obtain elsewhere. Controlled property can even be freed from control if it is brought up to standard, which eventually means for the landlord the far higher rents permissible under the rent regulation scheme.

But all that the local authority can oblige the landlord to do is keep his property dry and safe, to a fairly minimal public health standard, and, if the matter comes to its attention (which is rarely), keep the number of tenants below the statutory overcrowding standard of one and a half persons per room, counting small children as half a person and babies under six months not at all.

If the structure of the private sector were different, obligation might not be necessary. But it is characterized, as the Milner Holland report has shown, by a huge number of very small landlords, many of them old women owning only one house, who regard their property as a useful source of income rather than a business and prefer to avoid bother rather than to maximize their return. Since the report, there has been evidence to suggest that the few who do operate along businesslike lines have now shrewdly concentrated their holdings in the unregulated furnished sector, where they can make an ample income without going to the trouble of satisfying any public authority. If this sector ever came under regulation, they would probably leave property altogether – as they have largely moved out of unfurnished lettings – and invest their capital in some other field with a higher return.

Thus, although landlords own a third of London's houses, including almost all the large and shabby ones, and house close on 40 per cent of its households, they account for a minute proportion of the paltry 6,000 improvement grants given annually in the London area or the 2,500 new dwellings created by conversion. What improvement takes place is done largely by owner occupiers, with some grants taken up by local authorities themselves: the conversions are carried out by housing associations and, again, the local authorities.

The ingenious GLC idea of taking seven-year leases on landlords' property, carrying out the work, then returning it for the landlord to reap the benefit of higher rents, could make an immense difference to the situation. So could the adoption by other councils of Lambeth's readiness to help owners of rent-controlled property in need of renovation. This particular borough has been prepared to rehouse a tenant, who may then qualify for a rebate, before applicants queueing on the waiting list. The house is then freed for proper conversion (with the help of grants) and the owner can charge fair rents immediately, a much greater incentive to act than the official five-year phasing operation. All the council wants in return is the right to nominate one letting, or however many households it has provided homes for. But it also knows that one less building is going to become a slum. Yet, in the last resort, there is no way of compelling a landlord to cooperate. Nor is there any guarantee that the property will remain in good condition. The increasing number of housing associations are already making a difference. But their role depends on landlords being willing to sell to them.

It's hard to be optimistic. And it's very revealing that the Standing Working Party has very little optimism either. It sees the number of improvement grants rising from 6,000 a year to no more than 7,000 within the next five years. Nor does it see the 2,500 units created by conversion rising to more than 3,000 in the same period. Since, by its own definition, there will still be a minimum shortage of up to 156,000 houses and flats and up to 342,000 unsatisfactory houses at the end of five years, this rate of progress is ludicrously inadequate.

Still, if the rate were faster than this, at some point the second obstacle would become critical. This is the extensive poverty that exists in London – concentrated particularly, at the present time, in the private rented sector. London's average income is, in fact, the highest in the country. At £34 a week in 1968, it was fully 20 per cent above the national average of £29. What this average conceals, however, is a polar situation with the highest incomes in the country at one end and a unique concentration of low-paid workers in old-fashioned industries and the service sectors at the other.

At the top, in 1968, London had a third of its households with over £40 a week (compared with 20 per cent for the nation) and as many as 10 per cent with over £60 (5 per cent nationally). At the bottom, however, were a quarter of all households with under £20 a week. The average income for this group was under £12 a week, although only a third of them were retired. Just above this were a further 11 per cent with £20–£25 a week, average income £22 14s., and almost none of them retired. These incomes were only as high as this, moreover, because of extensive working by wives and by people over sixty-five.

What makes the position of these groups particularly difficult is the high proportion of high-income households, given the competitive housing situation. Housing carries a high price in London, in part because of the physically limited stock, but in part too because it is an area of great attraction to certain highly paid occupational groups. Even the average Londoner is hit by this, for while his income may be 20 per cent above the nation, his housing costs are 50 per cent above.

For London's poor, the situation is disastrous. While the average London household still only had to put 15·6 per cent of its income towards housing in 1968, the under £20 group put 28 per cent. This is fantastic when one considers that it included a sizeable council sector paying a subsidized rent (27 per cent of the group) and must have covered many households in receipt of rate rebates. Those in the £20–£25 group were only a little better off: for them the proportion was 18 per cent.

High as the proportion of income is, however, the more revealing figures are the distribution of the poorest by housing sector and the amount they actually paid for their accommodation. In all, 40 per cent of the bottom group and about 42 per cent of the next were in privately rented housing, a higher proportion in both cases than were in council housing. Secondly, although regulated rents in the private sector were running at a level about 80 per cent above council rents at this time (according to GLC research) and unregulated, uncontrolled rents at a level above that, this is only reflected in the amount the furnished tenants paid. The remaining private tenants in the poorest group paid

substantially less and in the next group slightly less than the council tenants. In other words, they were pretty certainly occupying the worst accommodation in the private sector: either controlled accommodation, which is virtually substandard by definition, or rooms within a multi-occupied house.

The coincidence of the poorest with the worst private housing shows up at the other end too. In the Government's Housing Survey in England and Wales, carried out in 1964, it emerged that no less than 60 per cent of the tenants in shared private accommodation were in the Registrar General's social categories III (manual), IV and V (the working-class categories). About 33 per cent were in categories IV and V. Among controlled tenants sharing, the proportions were 69 per cent and 38 per cent.

Since improvement cannot be achieved without some increase in rent, the drive to accelerate it has serious implications for the 400,000 households (more than 14 per cent of all London's households) who are in the two poorest categories and in privately rented accommodation. The extension of some rent assistance to them, desirable in any event, becomes absolutely essential in the light of this objective. Without it, in fact, the resistance of tenants is likely to bolster up the existing resistance of landlords.

But rent assistance, by itself, will not carry out improvement work. Indeed, by itself, it might not even improve the housing opportunity of those poor households with less housing than they need. For their chance of finding something better, in the absence of more units of accommodation, is limited by their ability to compete with younger, richer adult households. Their position will only clearly be better if the accommodation to suit them is available and if they are given some kind of priority claim on it.

Ideally, most families in their predicament – especially the elderly and families with children – should have a council house. Not because of the subsidy, since this would be largely irrelevant against a universal rent aid scheme. But because the public sector does guarantee something suitable and is flexible enough to allow further moves, as family circumstances alter, so that the accommodation always does remain more or less suitable.

Unfortunately, London begins with an unusually low stock of council housing by the standards of other cities – only about 20 per cent of all provision, compared with 30 per cent nationally. It is adding to this only very gradually about 20,000 units a year. Because of the low turnover and losses due to sales, the immense numbers on the waiting lists (about 190,000 at the present time) and the priority given to those in redevelopment areas, the chances of a poorly housed family with a low income obtaining one, unless it is in dramatically sordid straits, are low.

Much of this situation, however, stems from two character- istics of this sector which need not remain true: the financial advantage which a council tenancy possesses over all other kinds of accommodation and, secondly, the concept of the council house as a new-built unit. If rents did move to, say, cost-rent levels, while assistance was given through rebates only, much council housing would become – for those with high incomes – merely rather expensive modern accommodation. This might well speed up the exodus into owner occupation.

This process would, however, have to be handled with care – because there are far more tenants with middling than high in- comes, as the Prices and Incomes Board has shown, and it does take at least £36 a week in steady income, plus some capital, to buy the cheapest decent house in the London area. Unless cheaper, but equally acceptable, alternative accommodation were available within the London council system for them, cost rents might simply drive more of these middling-income tenants out of London altogether. The social balance has suffered enough from the exodus of social class III, manual and non-manual alike, for this to be contemplated with equanimity.

It also seems rather unfair that succeeding generations of ten- ants should meet the whole cost of housing that would never have been built if a cost-rent system had been contemplated. There is much to be said, therefore, for continuing to pass on directly the funds that come by way of expensive site subsidy and high build- ing subsidy.

Above all, a change like this would make it really imperative, from the council's financial point of view if from no other, to expand the proportion of its housing that can be rented cheaply. This ties in with the second point, for while it is virtually impossible to build cheap accommodation now without abandoning standards, it is possible to acquire it, particularly in the older areas. There have been steps in this direction, but usually for other reasons – for example, to house families temporarily while rebuilding took place.

If councils were prepared to buy extensively into the existing stock, a number of log-jams might be shifted. For a start, where improvement and conversion were lagging to an extent that needless waste of housing was taking place, an offer could be made for the property. This might not attract any more landlords than would be attracted by the seven-year lease idea. Indeed, the only answer to this one may finally have to be making neglect a ground for compulsory purchase.

What buying would do, however, would be to enable the house to be altered in the most appropriate way – into larger units, perhaps, than result from commercially motivated conversion (which would, in turn, help to stem the exodus of families with children). The council would be free, moreover, to sell this accommodation at a later date (assuming that councils would, by then, be permitted to sell flats, which is a reasonable assumption). This might be the answer to the problem facing middling-income tenants in a cost-rent situation.

Buying would also facilitate the redistribution of London's population from the congested inner area to the outer. The purchase of individual houses, as they came on the market, would augment the stock of accommodation suitable for large families in the worst areas, who come off very badly at present. The purchase of a number of adjacent houses in low density areas would make it possible to redevelop the land they occupy as flats. This in turn might tempt some of the elderly households living in five-room houses in the outer area to move to such flats, since it would enable them to stay in the same district.

This raises the prospect of a gargantuan council sector – in the early years, at any rate, before systematic selling to individual purchasers could be undertaken. But before one reacts with distaste at such a prospect, one should consider what a council tenancy will mean if changes like the introduction of universal rent aid and of rents related to value take place. It will less than ever mean housing reserved for one social class. It could, in fact, bring more help to London's white-collar workers than reserving corners of the redevelopment areas for privately owned housing. For the cost of such housing is so high that it ends up, inevitably, in the hands of the social class I and II groups – and often only the second-generation class II group, unless the individual belongs to one of the more highly paid professions.

The council's role will have altered, in short, from being the owner of a category of housing to being an agency of change. The actions it takes will be determined by housing need, in the broad sense, rather than individual need, and by planning considerations like the character of the area.

It will inevitably mean remaining the owner of many houses, perhaps the majority of all London's houses, in order to achieve these objectives. But London has always been overwhelmingly an area of tenants: the only difference will be that more of these tenants will pay their rent to a public authority. There is also a risk that the quality of management will deteriorate where immense numbers of tenants are involved. This is, however, a risk already. The answer to it, then as now, is greater decentralization and far more participation by tenants in the running of their housing affairs.

In all this, one crucial aspect of the situation has been ignored – the division of power between the GLC and the boroughs. The argument has proceeded as if there were only one public authority in the London area, with full control over every aspect of the situation. Perhaps this is as it should be, since the strategic role the GLC is expected to play requires a degree of cooperation from the boroughs that can never be assumed – and has not, in practice, been forthcoming. It has ended up playing a compensatory, instead of the strategic role the London Government Act envisaged (though this showed small understanding of the nature of the problem when it carved up the power structure as it did, as the Cullingworth report succinctly pointed out).

Certainly the proposals coming forward for other conurbation areas while the reform of local government has been discussed put the overall authority in a position of much more power. Both the Redcliffe-Maud and Derek Senior prescriptions for the rest of England give all housing policy decisions, except management, to the upper tier. In the Scottish Wheatley report, housing is to be handled at the planning region level – though, admittedly, Scottish planning regions are mostly smaller than English ones. This report places the entire responsibility for housing at this upper level, tempered only by decentralized administration.

One would hope that the occasion of reform elsewhere will be used to bring the London structure into line with that of other metropolitan areas on this count, if no other. For the time being, one can only urge that the GLC take no step in the direction of altering the rent and rebate situation until a common plan has been hammered out with the boroughs, to be implemented by all of them, which is supposed to happen in any event as part of the reform of housing finance. Even before this hurdle has been cleared, however, it should be pressing ahead with a policy of acquiring additional housing by purchase – both in the most rapidly deteriorating parts of the privately rented sector in the inner area and in the more thinly populated outer areas. This is the only sure and rapid means of diminishing the problems.

Jobs are the key to London's development. As the Greater London Development Plan says,

Location of employment is one of the most formative factors in planning [para. 4.6].

Yet the task of analysing and predicting the pattern of employment in London has been dogged by lack of information and tardy action, ever since the Barlow Commission in 1940 failed to take account of the growth of offices, and thus left planners unprepared for the office boom of the 1950s.

London's employment pattern is complex. Manufacturing industry, offices, hotels, shops, universities and many other institutions all make demands upon the labour force. Some of these demands are growing. For example the demand for hotel accommodation in London is expected to grow by anything between 60,000 and 250,000 extra beds by 1980, thus requiring a massive increase in the labour force. Other sectors of employment such as manufacturing are shrinking relative to the overall picture. It would be impossible to do justice to such a complex picture in a short chapter, and so I shall concentrate upon a particularly striking facet of London's growth in the post-war years which seems likely to dominate the scene for the next few decades – the growth and location of office employment.

Since the war the employment structure of London has been dominated by office jobs. This is true of the country as a whole. Between 1951 and 1961 office employment in the United Kingdom grew by some 1·2 million jobs, accounting for over 75 per cent of the total national growth in employment. By 1961 one in every three people employed in Britain did non-manual work. By 1966 the situation in London was even more biased towards office jobs. Within a work force of 4·5 million, some 1·5 million, or one third, worked in manufacturing industries, while nearly 3 million or some two thirds of London's jobs were in offices, shops and other parts of the 'service sector'. Approximately one half of these people, totalling 1·5 million, worked in central London.

Such background statistics are easy to understand, and indeed many of them form the basis of the Greater London Development Plan. Less easy to determine are the rates at which the figures are changing, and the interpretation we put upon the various rates of change which have occurred in London's employment structure during the post-war years.

Until the results of the 1961 Census were available it was assumed that London was confronted by a massive growth of office jobs, which were increasing at a rate of some 15,000 per annum. Policies were based on this trend and the dramatic figure was often quoted to back up the notion that too little was being done to avoid the unthinkable congestion which would result. For example, the LCC Development Plan First Review in 1960 said,

The number of people employed in central London seems to be increasing by 15,000 each year . . . almost twice as great as the rate for the whole of England and Wales.

Other commentators took up this theme. The South-East Study in 1964 said,

In the congested part of London – little more than the City and the West End – 15,000 more office jobs have been created every year.

The Town and Country Planning Association, in their pamphlet *The Paper Metropolis*, prepared in 1962, also reinforced this thinking,

In London's central area, the number of jobs in the last decade has grown by at least 15,000 a year. This increase was almost entirely in office employment.

We must bear in mind that the Town and Country Planning Association were, as always, eager for ammunition in their long-term battle for dispersal from congested London. But whatever motivations lay behind the discussions the figure of 15,000 new jobs per annum, based on the Board of Trade's analysis, was accepted as a basis for policy. In 1964, using such figures and arguments, the Government took action. In the White Paper on Offices, published on 4 November, it announced a control of all new office development in the London metropolitan area. The Office Development Permit, or ODP, system, gave the Board of Trade control of office growth, similar to that of factories via the Industrial Development Certificate system, which had been operating since the war. This new legislation was used to create a ban on office development in London, since only offices of less than 3,000 square feet were permitted to escape from the control system. This 'ban' was later extended to the whole of the South East. At last, it was felt, the problem and spectre of congestion created by the massive growth of office employment in London which had plagued the City since the forties, and which had been the gap in the Barlow Commission's thinking, was dealt with.

When, in 1965, the results of the 1961 Census appeared they threw the situation into confusion. It then appeared that between 1951 and 1961 the average annual growth in London's employment had been less than 6,000 jobs or just over one third the rate upon which previous policies, thinking and planning had been based. The confusion was openly acknowledged by the GLC and the Standing Conference on planning in the South East. In 1966 the GLC produced a research paper on central London employment in which the revised figure was quoted,

Comparisons between the 1951 and 1961 Census data indicate that the total increase in numbers employed . . . over the 10 year period is only of the order of 56,000 . . . considerably less than the estimates of growth derived from other sources principally Ministry of Labour employment figures.

At about the same time the Standing Conference made the obvious comment that the latest figures undermined basic planning policies.

The analysis confirms the very considerable differences between the employment situation revealed by the Census and that deduced from Ministry of Labour figures. . . . Had the Census data been available when the South-East study was prepared significantly different conclusions about the trends in the region and proposals to meet them might have been made.

In an article in the *Journal of Transport Economics and Policy* (1967) Alan Evans carried the view forward to suggest that employment in central London might actually have *decreased*. Far from causing the rejoicing one would have imagined, this suggestion had the opposite effect. It seemed that the evils of growth were preferred to the prospect of no growth. Official planners now stressed the need to locate any further office sub-centres well beyond the commuting area to central London 'if the essential labour force of the centre is to be retained'. The wheel has turned full circle. Thus the GLDP *Statement* says,

Yet London is short of labour and studies of the population's age structure show that the proportion of people of working age will decline. This could have serious consequences for the vitality of London. . . . Unless plans are made to the contrary London could be faced with a fall of over 700,000 in its resident work force by 1981.

In this respect the plan is simply the latest in a long line of gloomy forecasts, about the employment structure of London, since the debacle of the delayed 1961 Census figures turned the planner's thinking on its head. Indeed one of the more bizarre upsets in the history of British planning has been the turn-around which the 1961 figures compelled. The only consistency seems to be pessimism. At first there was pessimism about the congestion which massive rises in employment would entail. Predictions of slow strangulation at the centre and massive commuter problems loomed much in the mind of London's planners during the late 1950s and early 1960s. More recently, a new brand of pessimism has grown up concerning the survival of London's work force and the need to retain the essential functions of the metropolis, even that there may soon be too few jobs of the right sort. What will happen when the next figures appear? Shall we see yet another set of policies vainly trying to catch up with events, or are our forecasts now informed by past mistakes, and to this extent more reliable?

Whatever the answers to these questions certain predictions about London's employment pattern are now available. These have informed the Greater London Development Plan, and the basis for its discussion about policies. What then does the plan offer in the face of such major shifts in metropolitan jobs?

First of all there is no longer any doubt that the Office Development Permit system is weak and ill-considered. It has been under attack for some time, and its days seem numbered. In *London 2000*, Peter Hall argues that even in the realm of Industrial Development Certificates, which have been operating since 1945, the effects of controls have been limited, largely because of the great number of small-scale increments of employment which have slipped through the control net. Clearly the same effect will operate in Office Development Permits, especially since the limit of exemptions has been increased from 3,000 square feet to 10,000 square feet. Moreover, even where firms have been forced to move out of central London due to lack of space, they have not gone very far. The Location of Offices Bureau has for several years noted that most firms who are willing to move from central London will not go more than 40–50 miles from the capital. Thus the *regional* employment situation in the South East remains unaffected by the 1964 ban.

And the effects of the system are not confined to the South East. They may have serious international consequences. David Gransby, in a recent seminar paper, suggests that the ODP system, by forcing up central area office rents and constraining the amount of floor space available, may affect Britain's relationship with Europe. Office rents in the City of London may range from £14 to £27 per square foot, many times those of other European cities, as shown by the following table.

European Office Rentals – City Centre
(per sq. ft. per annum)

Paris	£4 4s. 0d.	to £7 10s. 0d.
Frankfurt	£1 1s. 0d.	to £1 14s. 0d.
Brussels	£1 5s. 0d.	to £1 14s. 0d.
Antwerp	£1 0s. 0d.	
Amsterdam	£1 5s. 0d.	to £1 14s. 0d.
Geneva	£1 5s. 0d.	to £2 2s. 0d.

(Source: Gransby 1970)

Such vast differences in office rents must surely affect the thinking of major international companies, when deciding where to locate a European headquarters. Thus, although the high rents of central London offices cannot be attributed solely to the ODP system, the effect is harmful at local, regional and international levels.

Perhaps the most comprehensive attack on the Office Development Permit system was mounted by Professor David Denman in *The Times* in July 1970. Denman demonstrates that, whatever the overall trends in London's employment may be,

Demand for office sites in London is a demand which by its very nature cannot be directed elsewhere nor lessened by failing to meet its importunity: and a feeble or non-existent demand cannot be generated by creating a profligate supply.

According to Denman, rental values in the City for modern offices have risen by some 380 per cent since 1965, while those of renovated pre-war offices have risen by some 280 per cent over the same period. These figures compare with rises of 40 per cent and 23 per cent respectively in places like Manchester and Liverpool. In real money terms these increases represent a jump from £2 10s. per square foot to £10 per square foot for new premises in the City. And these are only average rises. In the choicest some rents may be between £20 and £30 per square foot. Such high rents force out smaller professional offices from the central area. These activities have always been a major source of strength in the City of London and their presence is essential to its function. They cannot, therefore, move far and tend to settle in poorer-quality premises on the fringes of the City. Here they create new congestion problems as professional office workers and others seek to maintain their links within and across the central area. Indeed, it is this question of linkages, so familiar and so little understood, which is at the heart of London's problems. It could be said that there never has been an 'office problem' as such, only a linkage problem. The interconnectedness of London's activities is so rich that it is all but impossible to separate one set of activities from another. The Greater London Development Plan recognizes that the Office Development Permit system is an inadequate apparatus, and that, when it expires, as seems likely in 1973, it must be replaced by a more positive planning tool.

The special restriction on the building of offices imposed by the Office Development Permit system has prevented developments which could have caused a runaway demand for office workers in London. But the modified demand remains persistent, and the Council's policy is that it should be met to the extent that it can, for those activities which need to be located in London, within the context of a declining labour supply overall [para. 4.14].

The plan's proposal is to base the granting of an Office Development Permit upon a productivity measure, related to national employment patterns.

In addition the considerations governing the grant of particular planning permissions need to include the question whether a location in London will enable a project to contribute more to national objectives, such as increased output, than if it were located elsewhere [para. 4.7].

The criteria for such decisions are still being worked out, but some idea of the way things are going can be had from the plan's *Report of Studies*, and from a recent paper by Dr Frank Little, a member of the council's staff.

It seems that the measure of productivity for offices will be based on the criterion of 'relative net output per worker'. Now such a measure is easy to apply in the case of manufacturing industries, but there are a number of difficulties so far as offices are concerned. Data will be collected by the Business Statistics Office. Productivity of office work is notoriously difficult to measure, and at present the only proxy proposed seems to be the managerial to clerical staff ratio: firms with a higher ratio of managerial to clerical staff being regarded as more tied to London. Such an assumption seems suspect. For example, there may be radical differences between different kinds of firms. Professional firms, advertising agencies and finance houses may each have different managerial to clerical staff ratios, but this does not *necessarily* mean that one kind of firm is more closely tied to London. Indeed if such ratios are used as a basis for withholding or granting permission to remain in London, such a system might lead to 'cooking the books'. One can imagine a condition in which a firm wishing to stay in London would promote some staff from clerical to managerial level. These measures are still being tested, and one hopes for some less crude basis for taking such vital decisions about London's future. Nevertheless the productivity measure is a start, and is at least positive rather than negative in its effects. It does mark a step forward from the purely preventive measures of the Office Development Permit system.

But within such a policy what locational strategies does the plan suggest, and what will be their effect upon the face of the metropolis? Here one feels let down. True the plan does suggest a broad strategy for the location of jobs in London. It suggests more housing in London, better transport facilities for the journey to work and the allocation of new office floor space, based upon six main geographical sectors of the GLC area.

In fact the plan suggests an increase in office space in central and inner London of about 4 per cent, and an equivalent increase of between 10 per cent and 12½ per cent in the outer areas. Clearly some decentralization policy is at work, but is the strategy merely 'trend planning'? At a more detailed level the plan is careful to say that consultation with the local boroughs is necessary before any detailed strategy can be drawn up for particular areas. Yet just such detailed strategies are needed if the plan is to be a positive planning instrument. Some useful recommendations are made about the kind of criteria which might be used in deciding upon particular office locations:

What benefits will a particular project bring to a particular district? How will it fit in with other buildings planned in the area, with roads and with car parking? What contribution can it make to the restricting of London? What assistance can it give to larger developments of which it could form part? How is it placed for workers to reach it? [para. 4.21]

All good sound sense, if difficult to measure. But nowhere do we find an assessment of the actual impact on the shape of London or even parts of London. Perhaps this is because the planners have not been able to look beyond their own statistics, and the trends which these seem to spell out. Exciting long-term speculation is missing. If one does look ahead one may see significant changes in the distribution of office employment, which can affect profoundly the shape of the city. Perhaps the planners should do so. What are these trends?

First, the growth of offices is not peculiar to London. It is a feature of many other cities. The new plans for Paris show office towers rising over the city, and in Moscow great office buildings dominate much of the scene. The changes in society which give rise to such growth seem universal and continuing. Certainly there are no signs of the demand for offices falling off.

But perhaps the office function will become sub-divided. Parts will need to remain clustered closely together in the centre, while others may be dispersed or diffused, according to the residential patterns of office workers. For the time being it seems likely that London will continue to exert its pull. The central clustering of London's office activities will remain the most important single element in the country for the exchange of money, ideas, and information – the invisible 'transactional society', which will become even more dominant between now and the year 2000. The sheer number of offices and office jobs which already exists in central London assures it of a dominant position for several decades to come. What is more, the *image* of London as a unique city still attracts 'ideas men' and 'ideas industries'.

For London *is* a capital city, as well as being one of the world's great ports, and the financial, business and political heart of the country. There is no equivalent in the United States and very few anywhere else in the world. In the long run such a peculiar dominance may be unbalanced and will wither away, but in the short term it is unlikely to be swept aside.

But further ahead there may be big changes in store. Since the heart of the office function is in the exchange of messages, two things seem possible. First, routine messages and instructions can be automated. As a consequence, routine office functions may move out into suburbia, where the labour force is handy. But as automation takes over, the need for labour will diminish, leading again to more freedom of location.

What about the other part of the office function – the managers and the 'elite decision makers'? Such people need to communicate for two reasons. First, on matters of emergency, when a quick joint decision is needed to regulate production, marketing and so on. Second, when broad strategies for the future are being planned. In the first case, individual communication, via television or videophone, may enable the elites to carry out most of their work from home. Of course it is not known whether the 'elites' will *want* to conduct their business from home. The excitement and bustle of the city has great attraction and may overcome the discomforts of pressure, overcrowding and commuting. For matters of taste and fashion 'different strokes for different folks' is an imponderable which upsets the best-laid forecasts. However in the future the possibility of an elite of isolates is there and cannot be dismissed. In the second case, the need for conference centres could replace business districts. And as the affairs of the world become ever more interlinked, the location of these meeting places may change. The importance of some cities will decline while others will move up the scale. The development of South America or Japan may lead world attention away from Western Europe. In the long run, Africa and South-East Asia may become primary nodes in the world network of transactions. Such global changes may be complemented by the growth of new city centres at airports, hoverports or other communications interchanges.

What are the consequences for London? Clearly planners must balance the tendency for office employment to diffuse, spread and drain away from the centre against the continuing role of London's central area as the focus for national development.

The kind of metropolitan area needed must enable the centre to retain its hold while providing for a new system of other centres, located at some distance from the traditional heart of the city, and linked to each other, to the centre and major communication interchanges. The plan sketches in such a system, and suggests a system of roads and suburban centres for development, although the two do not always coincide. But more specific plans are needed, and needed quickly if the plan is to seize the imagination. The clash of interests between the London boroughs and the GLC is partly responsible, for the plan is so careful to stress that nothing can be done without consultation. But even so it is a bit vague, and one wonders upon what *specific spatial* issues such consultations will be based.

Let us take the three major areas in which office employment will occur: the centre; the suburban areas; and the South-East region, beyond the metropolitan fringe.

First the central area. Here restrictions on office building should be guided by more positive policies. Because of the ban on new development many residential, university and other areas are being invaded by small offices, forced out by high rents. In some cases, as in the eastern and north-eastern fringes of the City of London, such changes may be beneficial, but in others, such as Bloomsbury, the changes are often for the worse. The places to encourage office development are obvious – around the main line rail termini.

Most of London's rail termini and some underground stations, particularly on new lines, could serve as appropriate locations for offices, and the central area would be ringed by a pattern of office development complementing the City and West End, and siphoning off the pressures which are at present invading inappropriate locations. Allied with such a policy should go improvements in transport, to retain and help the commuter workers. Such improvements could be helped by a policy of locating central office growth at main line termini.

Next, the suburbs. The GLDP indicates certain suburban centres, such as Wood Green and Ealing, as appropriate for major development. The trouble is that they do not all measure up to the Council's own criterion of good access for workers. Other centres, such as Willesden junction, or even Watford, might be better. Nevertheless suburban centre development is one of the keys to a successful office policy for London. Transport routes to these centres must enable trips around the periphery of the built-up area as well as to the centre. Perhaps the ringways will work, but public transport – improved bus services – must take the brunt of the journey to these suburban centres.

Finally what should be done about the outer areas – beyond the fringe – where the greatest growth can be expected? Here there are a whole series of towns – new and old – which afford opportunities for office employment. The older towns may well be in balance, as far as employment is concerned, and may not need more jobs. Yet there are towns, for example Reading and Aldershot, which are growing fast, here surely the plan should be broadened and made more specific in its employment proposals. The fact that it cannot, because of the planning fence set up around built-up London, only highlights the contradictions of legally trying to separate the capital from its region. And the new towns have suffered for years from an imbalance – too many manual jobs and too few offices. Surely some of the continuing rise of office jobs should be directed here – *pace* the efforts of the Location of Offices Bureau – but they have been working without a *plan*.

And one more point. All these developments – in the centre, in the suburbs, and in the outer area – must be connected to London's airports. Particular decisions may have to await a final decision on the third airport, but the principle remains – offices mean communications, and communications mean airports.

From all this it emerges that the chances of using office *growth* as a spur to the less fortunate regions of Britain are slim. For most of the activities which contribute to the function of the

City, and thus add so much to our invisible exports, a central location is paramount. To relocate even part of the City's functions would entail national costs far above any regional benefits. This partial view of London's employment problem illustrates some of the difficulties and opportunities confronting the planners. What is needed most of all is a long-term vision, backed by positive policies.

Shopping and Suburban Development

John Blake

After all the criticism that has been levelled against them in the past, it may perhaps come as a surprise to discover that the much-derided 'suburbs' are not only alive but flourishing. Yet this is indeed the case. In London, as in most other large European or North-American cities, the suburbs are gaining at the expense of the central business area. Many activities which had formerly been regarded as particularly appropriate to the city centre are now moving out, either to the suburbs or away from the city altogether.

This trend towards the dispersal of central area functions is evident, for example, in respect of office employment. Despite the boom in office building which preceded and indeed brought about the Control of Office and Industrial Development Act, 1965, the number of office workers employed in central London fell marginally by about 5,000 between 1961 and 1966, whereas in the remainder of inner London there was an increase of 28,000 (+10·4 per cent) and in outer London an increase of 108,000 (+28·3 per cent). During this period numerous firms either moved their offices wholly out of the central area or 'hived off' their more routine office functions to new premises in the suburbs where rents were lower and labour (especially female labour) more readily available. Nor is there as yet any sign of this process coming to an end. The GLDP *Statement* declares that future policy will be 'to stimulate [office] development in outer London' and estimates that between 1966 and 1971 the amount of office floorspace in outer London will rise by 10·4 per cent as compared with only 3·9 per cent in central London. Moreover, these estimates were prepared in the context of the Government's policy of restricting office construction throughout the whole of Greater London. As the Location of Offices Bureau remarked in their *Annual Report for 1969–70*, 'there is no lack of interest in decentralization, and the scope for a considerable outflow is there if only there were an adequate supply of offices to accommodate it.'

As well as offices, there has also been some dispersal of routine wholesaling and distribution activities. The most striking examples are the pending relocation of Covent Garden Market at Nine Elms, Battersea, and of the Brentford and Stratford Markets on new sites further out, but equally significant has been the more unobtrusive exodus of a number of private wholesaling firms from long-established premises in central London.

Finally, there has been a steady decentralization of shopping activity. For some years past the trade of shops in central London has been growing at a slower rate than that of shops situated in the suburbs. Between 1950 and 1961 the rate of increase in the retail trade of central London shops was less than half that of the outer London shops, and this trend is expected to continue. In the GLDP *Report of Studies* it is forecast that between 1961 and 1981 their turnover will increase by 22·6 per cent and 50·3 per cent respectively, and the GLDP *Statement* further estimates that between 1966 and 1981 the amount of shopping floorspace in central London and the West End will rise by 3·2 million square feet (+3·5 per cent) as compared with 9·1 million square feet (+14·6 per cent) in outer London. This dispersal of shopping activity is due partly to changes in the size and distribution of the population but mainly to people spending proportionately more of their money in their local shopping centres.

One of the main planning problems now facing the suburbs, and especially the outer suburbs, is how to respond to the pressures resulting from this process of decentralization. Where should the new offices and shops be located? Should they be concentrated in a few major centres, or dispersed more widely throughout the area? This is a matter of particular concern to the London boroughs because it is they who will have to prepare the local plans which will determine the form of the new development and how it is to be fitted into the existing settlement pattern.

The GLC's answer to this question is that the activities to be decentralized from central London should be re-concentrated in a number of selected suburban town centres. In the GLDP

Statement they defined twenty-eight existing centres as being of 'strategic' importance. These were mostly the larger of the suburban shopping centres (usually with a retail turnover of at least £5 million in 1961), although other factors such as their position and relationship to other centres, their accessibilty and lines of communication, and their shopping prospects in relation to the future distribution of the population, were also taken into account. Of these 28 'strategic' centres, six were defined as being of 'major strategic' importance by virtue of their superior accessibility and drawing power – Croydon, Ealing, Ilford, Kingston, Lewisham and Wood Green.

The definition of a centre as being of 'strategic' or 'major strategic' importance was intended primarily to establish it as a focal point for future expansion. Thus a report on office policy recently produced by the GLC stated that 'concentration at a relatively small number of large centres with good accessibility is generally to be preferred to dispersion' and that the 'strategic' centres would be 'preferred locations for major office developments'. In the case of shopping, the GLDP *Statement* estimates that whereas the shopping floorspace of the twenty-eight 'strategic' centres will increase by 6·9 million square feet between 1966 and 1981 (+32·6 per cent), the floorspace of all other shopping areas outside central London and the West End will decrease by 3·6 million square feet (−4·0 per cent). As these figures imply, the 'strategic' centres are expected to capture trade not only from central London and the West End but also from other smaller 'local' shopping centres in their vicinity.

The philosophy underlying the GLC's policy was neatly summarized in *Tomorrow's London* as follows: 'We do not limit the right of Londoners to visit the West End. Instead, we encourage the growth of a number of "West Ends" on a smaller scale.' This approach has obvious merits, but it has to be remembered that these smaller 'West Ends' will not be new developments on virgin land but insertions into a built environment which derives its form from the social, economic and technological circumstances prevailing in the late nineteenth and early twentieth centuries. If the new 'West Ends' are not to suffer from the same disadvantages as now afflict central London, their development will have to be accompanied by a massive investment in their physical infrastructure – above all, in the improvement of their inherited road patterns

Already, most suburban town centres suffer from serious traffic congestion. Their narrow streets, frequent intersections and irregular alignments, their inter-mixture of conflicting vehicular and pedestrian movements, their lack of adequate off-street parking facilities and the impossibility of servicing the great majority of buildings other than from the street on to which they front – all these factors have combined to make them ill-equipped to cope with the increasing use of private cars for business, shopping and other purposes. What is more, the problem seems certain to become even more acute over the next ten to twenty years. The *London Transportation Study* has predicted that over London as a whole the total number of trips by all motorized modes of transport could rise by nearly 50 per cent between 1962 and 1986, while the number of trips for shopping and business purposes could nearly double. Moreover, not only will there be a substantial increase in the number of trips made daily, but there will also be a significant change in their mode of transport. Whereas in 1962 about a third of all trips were made by car drivers, and bus passengers were almost as numerous, by 1986 more than half the increased number of trips will be undertaken by car and only one sixth by bus. Thus the total number of car trips could more than double by the mid 1980s. While the realization of these forecasts depends upon an extensive programme of road construction and improvement, which may well prove difficult to implement within the given time period, they do give some indication of the extent to which vehicular traffic could increase over the next decade, and in particular that the greatest increases are likely to be in the form of short-distance trips generated by town centres.

To cope with the problems posed by the growing volume of traffic visiting or passing through town centres within their areas, the London boroughs have had recourse to various palliative measures. Traffic management schemes have now been introduced in many centres, involving the creation of one-way streets, the banning of right-hand turns, the diversion of through traffic along circumferential roads (often quite unsuited for the purpose) and the introduction of parking controls. These schemes have enabled the traffic to keep moving and sometimes even led to an increase in the average speed of flow, but frequently such gains have been counter-balanced by a resultant deterioration in the quality of the general environment. At the same time efforts have been made to provide more off-street parking facilities, and wherever possible opportunity has been taken of new development to segregate vehicles from pedestrians, either by the creation of pedestrian precincts or through the separation of functions on a vertical basis. However, it is fair to say that relatively little has so far been achieved by way of the structural reshaping of existing town centres, which is inevitably a long, costly and somewhat piecemeal process.

Since the relief afforded by the introduction of traffic management schemes in recent years can be of only temporary duration, and since there is little prospect of existing town centres being comprehensively redesigned and rebuilt over the next ten or twenty years, plans have now been prepared for most of the larger centres (as well as for many of the smaller ones) based on the principle that through traffic should be taken out of the central shopping and business areas through the construction of new by-pass roads, thereby enabling those central areas to become largely or wholly 'pedestrianized'. At the same time, rear access roads would be provided to service the shops and other buildings, and the number of off-street car parking spaces would be greatly enlarged.

Such schemes are probably essential if the larger 'strategic' centres are to cope with the traffic problems which will inevitably arise from their present functions, let alone the extra traffic which will be generated by their proposed expansion. However, they will also cost money. According to estimates published in the *Surveyor* in September 1969, the schemes already prepared for seventeen of the twenty-eight 'strategic' centres would alone involve an expenditure of some £85 million on roadworks, and if the schemes currently being prepared for the remaining eleven centres are taken into account the total could well amount to some £120 million by 1981. In most cases these schemes represent the minimum rather than the maximum level of investment considered necessary.

Unfortunately, few of these schemes stand any chance of being implemented. According to the revised road investment programme agreed by the GLC in January 1970, only £150 million will be spent on the 'secondary' road network between 1971 and 1981, as compared with £300 million (plus an undisclosed Ministry of Transport expenditure amounting to perhaps £100 million) on the 'primary' road network of new urban motorways. Since this £150 million will have to cover all improvements to the existing main road system, including the feeder roads to the new motorways and the entire road network in central London, it is clear that only a small part of it will be devoted to road improvement schemes in suburban town centres. Just how small a part it will be is evident from the first three instalments of the Ministry of Transport's *Preparation List* of schemes likely to be admitted to the firm construction programme within the five- to eight-year period beginning in 1971. Altogether the List includes fifty-five secondary road schemes costing an estimated £79 million, but only eleven of these schemes (costing £15 million) are in suburban town centres. On this basis, total road expenditure in the 'strategic' town centres is likely to amount to less than £30 million by 1981, as compared with a requirement of some £120 million.

There can be little doubt that the GLC's decision to devote such a large proportion of future road investment in London to the creation of a primary network of new urban motorways will leave little scope for the improvement of traffic conditions in suburban town centres. It is true that the new motorways will draw off much of the cross-London traffic which now passes through them, but such gains will be more than off-set by the increasing amount of short-distance traffic generated by them. The *London Transportation Study*'s own study of the likely effects of a proposed new motorway on secondary roads in the Wandsworth area found that, 'the environmental quality of the zone is already so affected by the traffic volumes as to be unsatisfactory in almost all respects; in 1981, it is predicted that the overall situation will be little changed, the increase in locally generated traffic largely counter-balancing the beneficial effect of the removal of almost all through traffic from the zone.' More recently, Professor Colin Buchanan observed in his report on *North East London* that 'in many, if not most of the shopping centres which straddle the links of the secondary road network the conditions are likely to be even worse than they are at present', and concluded that the problem 'is so gigantic that it seems almost beyond hope.'

There is some evidence that the GLC is belatedly beginning to recognize the extent of this problem. In *London's Roads – A Programme for Action* (November 1967) it declared that 'with so much demand for expenditure on the primary system, London will not be able to afford large physical improvements to [the secondary roads] except for very compelling reasons', and in the GLDP *Statement* it stated that 'town centres which do not contribute to the most important highway networks may have to wait'. However, in the draft report on *A Secondary Roads Policy* (November 1969) it accepted that 'it would be proper to allocate some investment specifically for road improvements in town centres in addition to any funds made available from those for secondary roads generally outside the central area,' while in July 1970 it accepted a Committee report which declared that 'it is not our intention that the allocation [of only one third of the GLC's capital investment on roads to the secondary network] shall be rigidly applied area by area or year by year . . . there will be flexibility in allocating the investment for secondary roads between the central area, town centres and the rest of London, with the possibility of some increase under the first two heads.'

Nevertheless, there is as yet no sign that the GLC has recognized the basic incompatibility between the planning and the transportation objectives of its plan. The decision to concentrate future shopping and office employment growth in selected suburban centres is clearly inconsistent with its decision to deprive those centres of sufficient funds to cope with existing pressures, let alone to accommodate further expansion. So long as the GLC remains committed to its current transportation policy, the appropriate planning policy ought logically to be one of dispersal rather than of concentration. Instead of attempting to create a number of smaller 'West Ends' in the suburbs, the aim should be to distribute future growth more widely throughout the area.

This is, in fact, what already seems to be occurring. According to the Board of Trade's *Census of Distribution* reports for 1961 and 1966, retail trade over both Greater London as a whole and the central area grew at almost exactly the annual rate predicted in the GLDP *Statement*. However, the trade of the larger inner London centres increased at only two thirds the rate forecast by the GLC, and of the larger outer London centres at only half the forecast rate. In the same way as the larger suburban centres have gained from the unsatisfactory traffic and environmental conditions in central London, so the smaller suburban centres now appear to be gaining from the steady deterioration of conditions in many of the larger suburban centres.

The moral of all this is not that the GLC's planning and transportation policies are necessarily wrong in themselves, but that considered together they cannot both be right. In present circumstances the logical corollary to a planning policy of suburban concentration is a much greater level of expenditure on the secondary road network than the GLC seems prepared to contemplate. It would inevitably involve a corresponding reduction in the scale or design standard of the proposed new motorways, or an extension of their construction programme (already expected to take more than thirty years to complete) over an even longer period of time. On the other hand, the logical corollary to a transportation policy which devotes the bulk of future road investment to the creation of a new motorway network should be a wider dispersal of shopping and employment activities away from the increasingly congested suburban town centres. This might in part take the form of new developments on or close to the new motorways, and the proposed new 'out-of-town' shopping centre at Brent Cross in Ringway 2 could well be a forerunner to other similar schemes elsewhere.

The GLC has said that its plan must be considered as a whole, but it bears all the hallmarks of having been compiled from a number of largely unrelated studies. In the same way as a collection of separately prepared regional plans does not necessarily constitute a sound national plan, so a collection of assorted subject plans does not necessarily constitute a sound urban plan. It is significant that in July 1969 the GLC amalgamated its Planning and Highways and Transportation departments in order to secure 'a unified approach to the problems of environmental planning, including communications.' Its plan for London might well have been a different plan, and perhaps a better plan, if this had been done four years earlier.

Transport: The Motorway Proposals

J. M. Thomson

Introduction

About 90 per cent of the objections to the Greater London Development Plan were registered against its transport proposals. These consist predominantly of a vast roadbuilding programme, designed to implant a network of motorways on the built-up face of London, and also to expand the traffic capacity of most of the existing main roads. The proposed motorway network includes three ring roads at approximately three, seven and twelve miles from the city centre (beyond which a fourth ring, outside the GLC boundary, is being planned by the Department of the Environment), together with about a dozen radial motorways or near-motorways mostly coming in as far as the inner ring (Ringway 1).

Ringway 1 will be largely overhead, although in some areas it will be sunk in a cutting. It will pass through dense residential areas such as Hackney, Camden, Hampstead, Fulham, Battersea, Lewisham and Greenwich, and will include about two dozen interchange areas where access roads and other motorways will curl in from all directions. Ringway 2 will pass through more dense residential areas south of the river, such as Streatham, Norwood, South Lewisham and Eltham, but north of the river it will consist mainly of the North Circular Road, duly widened and reconstructed. It will rise over the river at Barnes and dive under at Thamesmead. Ringway 3 will largely avoid housing areas but will take up large tracts of open space of various kinds. Ringway 4 will go mainly through open country. The radial motorways will be mainly along the lines of existing main roads entering London from all sides.

These motorways – roughly 400 miles of them – are to be known as primary roads. A further 1,000 miles of the current main roads have been designated as secondary roads and will be selectively widened to increase their carrying capacity by about 50 per cent. This work will cost half as much as the motorways themselves.

This, in a nutshell, describes the transport proposals. The plan contains no other concrete proposals of comparable importance – no major proposals for new or improved railway, underground or bus services, or for park-and-ride facilities or pedestrian precincts, or environmental areas. There are, however, suggestions that such things might be desirable, and since the publication of the plan the GLC has approved the construction of the Fleet line and the Heathrow extension. It is therefore possible that, given time, the GLC will supplement its road plans with programmes for improving public transport, pedestrian movement and the environment, even if these can only be achieved by sacrificing part of the roadbuilding programme. The GLC claims that its long-term planning policies are flexible and it has already shown this to be true on several occasions. It also points out with some justification that until the beginning of 1970 it had no executive responsiblity for public transport.

Nevertheless, while recognizing that the planning process at County Hall is a continuous, flexible process, and is not insensitive to reasoned argument and public feeling, the fact remains that the GLDP contains a gigantic transport plan which consists almost exclusively of roadbuilding. It thus represents fully the view that London's overriding transport need is for more and better roads.

This view will be examined in this chapter. Inevitably there will be numerous references to public transport, because one cannot sensibly discuss roadbuilding policy separately from public transport, but a fuller discussion of the future of public transport is reserved for the next chapter.

Production of a transport plan

The GLC has the duty to consider the future transport needs of the city and to produce a broad plan to meet those needs as fully as possible. It has little power to implement the plan, because it has no control over railways, it can do little roadbuilding without planning approval and financial support from the Government, it has very limited control over parking facilities and limited power to introduce environmental schemes. Although now in control of buses and tubes, it still relies on Government aid for capital investment. The council would clearly be failing in its duty if it produced a plan that lay entirely within its own power of execution. It must necessarily plan in consultation with the Government, the London boroughs, London Transport, British Rail and other bodies, in the hope that with their co-operation the plan may eventually be brought to fruition. It must in fact think and plan as an *overall strategic* planning authority even though it is far from being an overall transport authority.

There are four main steps in the logical production of an overall strategic plan:

1) Identification of the problem. What is the plan intended to achieve? What are the objectives?

2) Identification of alternative strategic plans for achieving the objectives, or at least making some progress towards them, subject to the severe limitations imposed by available finance, legal powers, public opinion, etc.

3) Prediction of effects of each alternative plan, on traffic, public transport, accidents, environment, parking, etc.

4) Evaluation of these effects in such a way that the plans can be rationally compared and the best one selected.

The controversy over the GLC's transport plan covers all of these four steps. Therefore each step will be discussed in turn in order to identify the points of conflict.

The conflict is not clear cut, however, being between two large, complex groups of people neither of whom are consistent in what they say and do. On one side is the GLC, a large organization containing inevitable differences of opinion between departments, between officials and politicians, and between political parties; the departments are being continually reorganized, the staff are continually changing, the political chiefs come and go. The arguments from County Hall change significantly from one year to the next. The statements of principle often seem at variance with the decisions taken.

The opponents of the transport plan, on the other hand, might be described as a large disorganization of residents' associations, civic societies, borough councils, members of Parliament, trade unions, the London Labour Party and others. Most of these bodies are in touch with each other, especially through the activities of central groups like the London Motorway Action Group and the London Amenity and Transport Association, but they nevertheless embrace a range of conflicting opinion and harbour a number of people with impractical and extreme views. Quite separate from these groups there is powerful, but discreet, opposition from British Rail, London Transport and from influential officials within government departments. It is impossible, therefore, to describe a single opposition view. Nevertheless there does appear to be some degree of consensus on the main issues.

The problem

There can be no doubt that historically the transport plan arose from a very great alarm at the growing traffic congestion on the roads. Ten years ago many people in authority still believed that traffic would 'grind to a halt' if nothing were done to provide room for the rapidly growing number of cars in London. The fear of a complete 'snarl up' led to the mounting – by the LCC and the government – of the great London Traffic Survey in 1962, with the initial purpose of collecting 'basic information on current traffic movements required for main road planning'. A team of highway and traffic engineers were set to work, who for several years devoted themselves almost exclusively to the problem of planning new roads to accommodate a vast increase in motor traffic. Only towards the end of the seven-year study (which became known as the London Transportation Study, or LTS) was any serious thought given to other aspects of the transport problem. A belated attempt was then made to study the needs of public transport, the effects of roads and road traffic on the environment, and the parking problem. But the road plans were already well advanced and were approved in principle by the GLC in 1966 when serious work was just starting on the other problems.

The GLC view at the time was clearly that the new roads were an essential and minimal requirement regardless of any further decisions that might be taken on matters affecting public transport, environment, or anything else. It was indisputable that car ownership was going to increase rapidly and that if the new car owners were to use their cars as much as did existing car owners there would be appalling congestion unless new roads were built, and built urgently. Despite the enormous cost, the disruption, the demolition of thousands of homes and the depressing prospect of huge superhighways distributing hordes of vehicles every day into every corner of London, there seemed no real alternative. The pessimists regarded it as the inevitable price of progress. The optimists thought that, by careful design and traffic management, the worst effects could be avoided.

To the opposition, however, this extreme anxiety about traffic congestion is seen as an obsession which blinded the GLC to everything else. Traffic congestion is only one aspect of the transport problem. Half the passenger-miles in London are carried by the rail network, on which passengers suffer worse overcrowding and slower overall travel speeds than do motorists. Worse still are the buses, which, it is argued, are much the most efficient users of scarce roadspace and should therefore be given priority over cars. The needs of the pedestrian also warrant far more consideration. The deteriorating condition of the environment seems to many people just as important as the fact that motorists have to queue up at traffic lights. Why, it is asked, are the authorities unconcerned if people stand for twenty minutes in the rain waiting for a bus, but willing to spend millions of pounds to save motorists sitting for five minutes in a traffic queue? There is also the question of road accidents: how can one ignore the fact that motor traffic is killing 800 people a year on London's roads and maiming thousands more? Surely this appalling fact must rank high among the problems to be tackled?

The opposition view, therefore, is that the GLC plan is

fundamentally misconceived, being based on a preoccupation with only one part of the transport problem. The GLC maintains, however, that the other parts have not been neglected and that the motorways will relieve not only traffic congestion but the other problems as well.

Alternative solutions

There is no scientific way of producing an optimal transport plan for a city. The original ideas must be largely intuitive and are bound to reflect the preconceived view of the problems to be solved. But once a plan has been formulated it can be rigorously examined against the facts, by a process of predicting and evaluating its effects. The only way, therefore, of ensuring that a good plan is eventually selected is to examine all the broad alternatives that seem feasible. The supremely important task is to hit on the right strategic plan: once this has been settled, a process of increasingly detailed modification can be embarked on.

There are not many real strategic alternatives in London. One possibility, involving much more than transport, is drastically to decentralize the city, moving a vast number of jobs right out of London and thus transforming the whole pattern of travel movement. There are several basic variations of this bold strategy, which do not appear to have received any detailed consideration. The GLC has decided firmly in favour of maintaining the broad land-use pattern in its present form, with a very strong central employment area surrounded by high density residential suburbs.

Given this decision, which is not disputed by many people, the alternative transport strategies are probably limited to the following:

1) Devote all available resources to roads, on the argument that people want to travel by car. This implies a comprehensive motorway network, since motorways are the cheapest way of providing new road capacity; the main alternative kinds of network are:

(a) a big radial network designed to maintain the predominance of the central area and to develop the corridor linkages that already exist;

(b) a big orbital network with radial connexions to the centre, designed to give maximum accessibility to all areas;

(c) a big orbital network without radial connexions to the centre, designed to stimulate the dispersal of activities throughout the suburbs at the expense of the central area.

2) Devote all available resources to public transport, on the argument that there is already too much private car traffic in London. This would imply not only an expansion of the public transport system but a radical improvement in its quality.

3) Expand the road network in the low-density outer areas and improve public transport in the high-density inner areas, on the argument that in the outer areas it is relatively cheap and easy to build roads and relatively costly to provide good public transport, whereas in the inner areas the reverse situation holds true.

4) Since all the above alternatives are exceedingly costly, one is bound to add the cheap alternative of leaving the system much as it is and forcing a reduction of road traffic in favour of public transport by management measures, e.g. restrictions on cars coupled with subsidized fares on public transport.

The above list is sufficient to show crudely that some major alternatives do exist. There may be others. But no real effort was made, during the preparation of the GLDP, to seek and examine any alternative strategy to that actually adopted, i.e. (1)(c) above. In particular, strategy (3) above, which is proposed by the opponents of the GLDP, was not examined.

In defence of the GLC it may be pointed out that the London Transportation Study was intended to develop and test alternative plans but the computer models proved so cumbersome and expensive that no realistic alternatives were ever tested.

Predicted effects of the GLC plan

It is not easy to predict the long-term consequences of implanting a large motorway network on London. One thing is certain:

the effects will be much more complex and far-reaching than most people realize.

The main purpose of the London Transport Study was to make just such predictions. By applying an elaborate forecasting programme in great detail to London, district by district, the London Transport Study predicted, on various assumptions, the future traffic, by volume, speed and composition (as between cars, lorries, etc.), on main roads, and movements by public transport. These predictions depend, of course, on the particular plan fed in to the programme. Only two strategically different plans, with some variations on each, were considered; these were known as Plan 1 and Plan 3. But Plan 1 could not be regarded as a serious plan; it represented minimum expenditure and contained Ringway 3 and a few stretches of radial motorway in the outskirts. It was intended to serve as a yardstick against which to measure the improvement produced by Plan 3. Plan 3 contained the full motorway network as originally proposed by the GLC.

It might appear at first sight that the London Transport Study predictions for Plan 3 provide just the information needed to judge whether the plan will have the desired results. But it is not as simple as that; both the GLC and their opponents claim that the London Transport Study predictions support their own case. The predictions show that if the motorways were built by 1981 the volume of traffic in London would then be about two and a half times its 1966 level, and half this traffic would be carried by the motorways. The existing roads would be fully loaded and carrying a lot more traffic than in 1966. Average traffic speeds would be significantly higher, mainly on account of the higher speeds possible for long-distance traffic, which would increase enormously.

The GLC claims that the motorways would thus remove a great deal of traffic from the existing roads, especially long-distance goods traffic. They also claim that the traffic situation on the existing roads would be improved as a result and that there would or could be a general improvement to the environment.

But there are many counter arguments. First it is difficult to reconcile the prediction that the existing roads would be fully loaded with the claim that both traffic conditions and environment would be improved. The GLC reply to this is that the situation on these roads would be even worse if the motorways were not built. But this is debatable since the roads would be carrying their full capacity anyway. The motorways, while drawing many traffic movements away from the secondary roads, would also generate many additional car trips which would inevitably start and finish on the other roads. Thus the motorways would take traffic away from the other roads with one hand but would put more back with the other.

Difficulties also arise from the fact that Plan 3 is not in fact the plan contained in the GLDP. Plan 3 included a considerable programme for public transport: new tubes, more trains, faster and better bus services, all at 1966 fare levels (relative to the cost of living). None of this is included in the GLDP, and fares have already risen sharply since 1966 as a result of the GLC's no-subsidy policy. Hence the LTS predictions of public transport movements are likely to be too high and the estimated shift from public to private transport too low. This is probably the weakest point in the whole GLC argument. One of the main reasons why motorways have so often failed to cure congestion in other cities is that they have sent public transport into decline. The loss of passengers leads to higher fares and reduced services, which leads to further loss of passengers. As more and more people give up public transport and take to their cars the new roads become congested, by which time public transport is no longer capable of attracting back its former passengers. The car owner is left with the choice between traffic congestion as before and an expensive, inferior public transport service. The non-car owner has to pay up and suffer. This has happened in many American cities. It is already beginning to happen in London.

Another difference between Plan 3 and the GLC plan is the time scale. For lack of money, the motorways are now not expected to be completed until the end of the century. The LTS target year was 1981. The implication is that for thirty years, while every available penny is put into the motorway programme, there will be a severe shortage of funds for all other transport projects. One is bound to ask whether there is not some faster, cheaper way of tackling the problems which are already present. Even if the motorways were worth having in 1981 it does not follow that they would be worth waiting for until the year 2000.

Another large area of controversy covers the LTS predictions themselves. Large sums of money spent on big computer programmes do not guarantee good results. The techniques of urban traffic forecasting are complex, expensive and perhaps daunting to the non-specialist. But there are many reasons for doubting their ability to produce reasonable results. The techniques used by the GLC and the LTS have been criticized on the grounds that, for numerous reasons, they fail to reflect adequately the power of new roads to generate traffic and conversely the power of congestion to limit the volume of traffic. These criticisms imply that the predictions systematically under estimate the amount of congestion that will arise if the motorways are built and over estimate the amount that will arise if they are not built.

Evaluation

Even if people can agree on the likely traffic results of the GLC plan there still remains the difficult problem of deciding whether these results are worth the immense cost and other sacrifices involved. The cost estimates have escalated and are now over £2,000 million, i.e. about £800 per London family. This figure covers the expansion of the secondary roads necessary if the motorways are to function effectively. In addition there are many social costs that cannot be measured. What price is to be put on the environmental damage caused (a) by the cutting of many miles of motorway through dense residential areas, parks, conservation areas, sports grounds and places of special beauty such as Greenwich and Cheyne Walk, (b) by the widening – to Finchley Road standard – of a large number of existing main roads, and (c) by the penetration of much larger volumes of traffic into most residential and shopping areas?

What price is to be put on the increase in accidents which will inevitably result from this large growth of traffic? The GLC points out that motorways are the safest kind of road, but if the existing roads remain fully loaded anyway the motorway accidents must be additional to those which would occur if the motorways were not built. It has been tentatively suggested that road deaths might rise by 500 a year.

The most hostile opposition to the motorways has come from the people who stand to lose their homes. This proves the obvious point that compensation at market value, plus removal expenses, is by no means adequate compensation for the hardship caused by eviction. If, as seems likely, about 100,000 people lose their homes, what price is to be put on the hardship caused? And what incidental costs will be imposed on the community in resettling all these people elsewhere, with the necessary provision of schools, roads, sewerage, water and power supplies, and other social capital not readily transferable from the areas in which they now live?

Another major imponderable is the loss inflicted on public transport, whether this is borne by passengers or by the community through a subsidy. The motorways are bound to lead either to a rise in the average cost per passenger-mile or to a fall in the quality of service, and this could be a large cost to the community.

The motorways and other associated road works, to be worth while, must produce enough benefits through their traffic effects to exceed all these formidable costs. But the evaluation of the traffic benefits is fraught with problems. It depends essentially on how successful the plan will be, not merely in relieving main road congestion but in speeding up door-to-door journey times. This raises the question of what happens to the motorway traffic when it leaves the motorways and tries to enter and park in London's 120 suburban centres. How much of the precious time saved on the motorway will be lost queuing up and trying to park in cramped little centres which are unable to cope with existing traffic volumes and need perhaps £1,000 million of redevelopment to enable them to deal with the predicted future volumes?

The GLC, of course, is trying to show by sophisticated calculations that the benefits will be great enough to outweigh all the disadvantages. But its benefit calculations are challenged at almost every point. One third of the total benefit is attributed to 'tax benefit', i.e. the benefit received by the Government in the form of extra fuel tax. This particular calculation is challenged on grounds of failing to take full account of tax losses on other commodities, e.g. alcohol and tobacco, the consumption of which will fall in consequence of higher expenditure on motoring.

Another third of the benefits is attributable to savings in leisure time, much of it at weekends. Here again it is claimed, by the opposition, that big errors have been made in the evaluation of leisure time and in the estimates of weekend traffic.

The remaining benefits are attributable partly to savings in the operating costs of private cars on leisure journeys and partly to savings to business trips and goods traffic. The growth rate of goods traffic predicted in the LTS has already been shown, in the years since the prediction, to be far too high. It is apparent that the benefits to business and commercial traffic comprise a very small part of the total. The case for the motorways rests overwhelmingly on their ability to enable car owners to use their cars more effectively for social trips and for driving to work in the suburbs.

Conclusion

Even if all the above arguments can be resolved and the GLC plan can be shown to offer benefits in excess of the costs, it still remains to be demonstrated that there is no better alternative plan. The opposition case is directed not against the whole plan but principally against two features of it: (1) the inner motorways, and (2) the neglect of public transport. Since there is insufficient money available to build all the proposed motorways *and* to embark on a radical improvement of public transport, it follows that the opposition plan is to abandon the inner motorways and spend more money on public transport instead.

The opposition groups unanimously reject Ringway 1 and the radial links between Ringways 1 and 2, but are divided over Ringway 2. Much of the fiercest opposition, however, comes from the areas in south London affected by Ringway 2. But even if only the former motorways were scrapped, and Ringway 2 was built to reduced capacity (say two lanes in each direction), something like £1,000 million would be saved. And this is precisely the figure required by the new investment programmes recently drawn up by London Transport and British Rail (for the London area).

The case therefore is crystallizing into a choice between providing inner London with a limited motorway system or a modernized public transport system. With the motorways, more people will use more cars for more and longer journeys; public transport will deteriorate and become more expensive; thousands of people will have to go and live elsewhere; those remaining will have to accept a formidable increase in noise, fumes, dirt, car parks, petrol stations and all the other by-products of motorization; main roads will be widened and turned into dual carriageways with consequent difficulties for pedestrians; the threat of accident will increase. Without the motorways, the people of inner London will have to learn to be more selective in the use of their cars; although the car will still be available for the journeys where it offers big advantages, for many other journeys public transport will have to be used; but public transport could be more extensive, more frequent, more comfortable; people will not be evicted from their homes, and the character and amenities of inner London will not be destroyed.

What kind of public transport system could be developed in inner London? What would modernization mean, and what would it cost? These questions have been left for the next chapter.

Transport:
The Two Cities
Terence Bendixson

How many Londoners have used the improved kinds of bus and underground services that have begun to appear in other cities in the past five years? In particular how many councillors and senior officials at County Hall have done so and how many are aware of the next generation of improvements that are on the way? If they have not experienced any of these changes and if their judgement of what is possible in the field of public transport is based on the buses and undergrounds of yesteryear, then they are likely to be making questionable decisions.

Among notable innovations there are some, like the carpeted trains with armchair seats due to start running under San Francisco bay in 1971, that are big and spectacular. Others, though no less important, are little things like the heated bus shelters at Pittsburg's Gateway Center; or an arrangement with local banks made by the Hamburg transport authority to save commuters the trouble of queuing up every month to buy a season ticket. Instead the banks post the tickets and debit the accounts of their customers.

Even more relevant to London are the lanes that have been reserved for buses and taxis over miles of streets in inner Paris. These have increased speeds by as much as three times over their previous levels and are being rapidly extended to try to improve mobility in a tight-packed city where the streets are clogged by cars flowing on and off new autoroutes and in and out of a warren of huge car parks.

A different but related kind of innovation is under way in the middle of Washington DC where a computer is due to be installed to operate the traffic signals and to give buses priority over other vehicles. Washington, like New York, has also started experimenting with closing some of its main shopping streets to cars. Strolling players have even been brought in to replace the roar of traffic. It has not been thought necessary to build bypasses for the dispossessed vehicles. They have been left to find their way along other streets.

In New York, the development of this new kind of city street has been taken a step further. Electric mini-buses mingle with the pedestrians and give rides to people going several blocks. Over the next few years it seems likely that this will happen more and more. Local city transport will increasingly be lifted out of the melee of the roadways, cleared of noise and smell, and set down amidst people on foot.

There is no hint of anything like this in the Greater London Development Plan. Instead the document exudes what critics of a similar attitude in Amsterdam call a 'car-window mentality'. An aspect of this is a belief that it is appropriate to drive urban motorways through cities irrespective of whether the streets and buildings are tight-packed or loosely-knit.

Victorian London and its more recent semi-detached surroundings are accordingly to be branded with identical ringways as if there was no difference between them. Yet if one had to choose one thing upon which the majority of critics of the plan are agreed it is that London – from Hammersmith to Hackney and from Streatham to Wood Lane – is a singular place that needs special treatment.

To be fair to the GLC it is clear that attitudes have changed since work started on the transport aspects of the development plan in 1960, and that they are changing still. It is possible to get a measure of this by comparing the various reports that have emanated from County Hall or been commissioned by it over the past five years.

The most antiquated thinking is contained in the studies that were done in the course of preparing the development plan. As ill-luck would have it the transport chapter of this report was greatly influenced by the work of a firm of Anglo-American consultants who were in turn heavily influenced by what was going on in United States cities in the late 1950s – the design of the built-on-the-cheap freeway systems that now snarl and snake through cities such as Chicago, Philadelphia and Detroit.

The result is a strong bias towards urban motorways despite their agonizing implications for peace and quiet, the prospect (as the studies say) that 'there will not be sufficient road space to allow all journeys by car' and notwithstanding an admission that even at some remote time in the future 'half the population will not have access to a car at all times'.

Somewhere along the line of reasoning the point got overlooked that although cars are a blessing when in the hands of only a few people, they become an unworkable proposition when multiplied indefinitely in densely built-up cities.

Nowhere is the GLC's car-window mentality so obvious as in a reference to the prospects for bus and coach services. 'Although a bus loaded with passengers makes more efficient use of road space than a private car, it cannot offer better travel time, comfort or convenience,' the studies say. This would, of course, be true for the hypothetical circumstances in which a single traveller by bus and a single traveller by car are pitted against one another in the open spaces of rural Lincolnshire. But in the 620 square miles of London, with over 7,500,000 potential travellers, plus their Home County cousins, it is not like that. Arguments can as easily be advanced to show that improved bus services offer a very promising way to speed Londoners on their way.

This was done by Dr F. V. Webster of the Road Research Laboratory in a report 'A theoretical estimate of the effect of London car commuters transferring to bus travel', published in 1968. He concluded:

The calculations suggest that any of the systems of buses within the range 20–70 seaters could adequately cope with the present passenger traffic during peak hours and could reduce the average journey time for all travellers combined by up to one third. Some, but not all, of the present car drivers would have longer journeys when travelling by bus, but others, as well as all present bus passengers, would have shorter journey times. Fares could be reduced with some of the systems which could at the same time provide a better service. Economically, the system applied to central London could result in a saving in vehicle-operating costs and passengers' time costs of up to £20 million per annum.

As might be expected the preoccupation with highway improvements so evident in the studies was carried into the statutory development plan, although this is not apparent in the
preamble. It says:

The Council's policy has the twin objectives of improving public
transport in all possible ways and developing the road system to
cater efficiently for the enormous amount of road traffic which is
essential to the proper functioning of London.

Yet such a two-pronged approach is never substantiated in the
plan.

When it comes to programmes of action there is a commitment
to the £2,000 million ringways system but bus users have to
content themselves with such statements as 'no longer can buses
be expected to be sufficiently flexible to run good services without
some special provision'. The nature of that provision is never
explained. Considering that the red buses daily carry about five
million passengers, more than the combined totals of the undergrounds (about 2 millions) and the railways (750,000) this is
surprising.

The authors of the plan were also acutely concerned with the
distant future – the hypothetical days of 'maximum car ownership' – and neglectful of the years leading up to it. Perhaps this
is inevitable in a long-term planning exercise, but in that case the
distant plans should at least be based on the understanding that
they will be affected by actions that have to be taken in the
interim. As it is, the long-term proposals of the highway engineers show no signs of being designed in the light of the major
improvements to public transport that will have to be made in
the 1970s to combat the effects of road congestion.

Furthermore the GLC's preoccupation with crystal gazing
seems to have caused it to overlook the significance of some of its
own figures. Examples are those describing the lives of Londoners in the 1960s. These show that seven out of ten families in the
old LCC area were without cars in 1962 and thus totally reliant
on buses, tubes and trains to get about. In other circumstances
these statistics might have signalled the need, on grounds of

social justice alone, for immediate action to improve such services and to give the buses in inner London priority over other
traffic.

But the signal went unheeded even though the forecasts of the
planners showed that the number of Londoners dependent on
public transport was not going to shrink suddenly into a tiny
minority. The council's own forecast was that about half the
families living in the inner boroughs north of the Thames would
be without cars in 1981 and that 46 per cent would be without
them in those boroughs to the south of it. But even in households
with a car there will be plenty of occasions when some members
will need to use public transport, particularly if the family Ford
or Austin is used by a breadwinner to go to work. Add all the
wives and children and elderly parents in these circumstances to
those without any access to a car at all and the absence of policies
for immediate improvements to bus and tube services becomes
even more puzzling.

Inevitably the GLC itself began to be aware of this situation
as a result of public outcry and possibly too as a result of feedback from the USA about the social discontents that bubble up
when public transport is left to decline.

There was even a reference to this in *Movement in London*,
the last volume in the GLC's transport trilogy, an indication that
it was not for lack of wide-ranging research that the transport
policy of the plan was so unbalanced. Summarizing a study by
Research Projects Limited, volume three says that when working-
class people are affected by delays, irregular running, route
changes and fare increases 'they feel and strongly resent their
helplessness'. In the United States a compounding of this and
other sorts of helplessness has been identified as a cause of urban
strife. Occasional outbursts of a similar kind in London hint that
it would be perfectly possible to cultivate comparable violence
here.

Worse still from the GLC's point of view, their own comforting words about the beneficial effects of the ringways on London's
old main roads have been thrown back in their faces by no less an
authority than Professor Colin Buchanan in a study *North East*

London, commissioned by the GLC. Describing the traffic conditions in Newham and Waltham Forest that will accompany the new highways, Professor Buchanan says:

We are unable to satisfy ourselves that the policy at present implicit in the plan will improve environmental conditions other than by a certain draining off of traffic from residential areas lying in the interstices of the network. Without wishing to belittle this particular gain, the fact seems to be that in many, if not most of the shopping centres which straddle the links of the secondary network, the conditions are likely to be even worse than they are at present.

This leads him to the conclusion that these much-thronged places should be by-passed or rebuilt. Yet he goes on to confess 'a feeling almost of despair' because financing another vast programme of public works on top of the £2,000 millions already committed seems too difficult. '. . . the problem is so gigantic that it seems almost beyond hope,' he concludes.

One way out of this predicament is the improvement of public transport. On this Buchanan says: 'Whilst improvements to main line and underground rail services will play a part, we think it is the role of the bus that will be crucially important.' But for buses to do their job cars must be kept in check and among the techniques recommended are parking controls, the provision of bus lanes, the subsidizing of bus fares, schemes to seal off residential streets from through traffic and the development of pay-as-you-drive road tolls.

Out of all this seems to be emerging a picture of inner London as a place where people and buildings are so thick on the ground that droves of cars can only be accommodated if the community is prepared to put up with extremes of danger, noise and fumes, or to finance the complete rebuilding of their surroundings.

A growing number of Londoners, having begun to appreciate the financial impossibility of accommodating cars in a civilized fashion, have come to believe that a completely different approach, based on giving priority to the improvement and development of buses, tubes, trains, taxis and hired cars, is necessary in the inner boroughs.

Professor Buchanan, though he stresses the importance of public transport, is not prepared to say it should have financial priority. Indeed he urges the GLC to spend yet more money on highways. He says that, in addition to building the ringways and their feeders, it will be necessary to upgrade many of the existing roads in order to ensure a tolerable environment as well as widespread opportunities to use cars. How much all this would cost and where the money would come from is a question he conveniently leaves unanswered.

Emphasis has been placed so far on London's roads and buses because, with the possible exception of the Northern line, that is where public transport is breaking down fastest. The buses are also such ubiquitous carriers. But there is another reason for concentration on road public transport. London's bus services are uniquely capable of swift improvement. They could be transformed almost at the drop of a hat, and at nominal cost, by giving the buses priority over other traffic and introducing off-peak fare reductions of the kind being pioneered in the Manchester area.

Such immediacy needs to be compared with the nine years it is estimated it will take to tunnel the Fleet line or the two years needed to get new trains into service on the Northern line. On the other hand, it is important not to dismiss the effect of changes to fares and frequencies and other administrative innovations in upgrading the services offered by undergrounds.

One measure of the importance of London's railways is that they account for 38 per cent of all mileage travelled and for as much as 50 per cent of it in peak times. The implication of this is, of course, that they carry people longer distances than other kinds of public transport. The authors of the plan dutifully looked at the rail network and their conclusion was that it was 'well suited to London's needs' though they went on to list a variety of improvements under consideration by British Rail and London Transport. There is no commitment to any of them beyond a general statement that 'the Council's objective is that the rail system must develop and improve to provide higher levels of service.'

The task of carrying this out is left largely to the railways and in December 1969 the Southern Region, which brings about 300,000 passengers into London every day, published a £220 million development plan for the 1970s. The two main items on this were new carriages with automatic doors, to be introduced at the rate of 200 a year, and a chain of thirteen power signal boxes serving the whole region. Modernization on this scale would mean spending £12 million a year more than the £10 million the SR is currently investing and there has so far been no sign from the Government that the additional money will be forthcoming. Yet if modernization is held only at its present level, commuting will be even nastier in the 1980s than it is today, according to Mr Lance Ibbotson, general manager of the Southern.

The development plan makes no reference to these conflicting demands for money and contains no information about the investment needed to keep the railways going. On the other hand the plan does commit the council to redeveloping Victoria Station, a project now in limbo following the decision to extend the tube and not the SR to Heathrow, and also to transforming King's Cross and St Pancras into a modern transportation interchange. Yet even this is linked to the possibility of a third London airport to the north east of the city, a prospect which now seems unlikely to materialize before the 1980s, if at all.

The plan is equally reticent about the future of the underground, though since its publication County Hall has become the proprietor of the tubes and buses. In this new role the council has said it will pay a quarter share of the £86 million Fleet line from Baker Street to New Cross via Fleet Street provided the Government pays the rest, and of a £17.7 million extension of the Piccadilly line to Heathrow. (This division of financial burdens was established by the 1968 Transport Act.) Decisions have also been made by the GLC to order thirty new trains to relieve misery on the Northern line, and to spend £1 million on modernizing South Kensington Station while a developer puts a hotel on top of it.

Taxis get an even briefer mention than tubes though the extension of radio to all of London's 8,000 hackney cabs, as well as to the fast-growing, unregulated mini-cab fleet, would increase productivity and bring benefits all round.

Hire-cars, though they could offer many of the conveniences of car ownership to residents of high density neighbourhoods and at the same time stem the proliferation of on-street parking and all the gutter-filth it entails, are not referred to at all.

It is hard to avoid the conclusion that the plan for London is partial and incomplete in its treatment of transport. To some extent, of course, this can be explained by the GLC's statutory obligations, to its lack of any managerial role in British Rail or the taxi industry, and to its very recent acquisition of responsibility for the tubes and buses. It has to be admitted too that the London Transportation Study, which started off as the London Traffic Survey way back in 1960, was a pioneering work and inevitably reflects the political and professional preoccupations of that time. Moreover the looseness of the subsequent plan means that there is room for manoeuvre.

Nevertheless when all is said and done the development plan alone is a statutory framework for the future of London. Any other documents are merely explanatory. Therefore it is the plan alone that must be judged. And it must be judged in the light of today's insights into the escalating cost of urban highways (£60 millions for the two-and-a-half-mile-long, four-lane, west cross route stretch of Ringway 1 behind Earls Court) and current feedback from the United States about communities divided by freeways and the growing resistance to them in cities such as Boston and Baltimore where conditions are akin to those in London. If the elephantine gestation period of the plan means that it was prepared before such things were common knowledge, all the more reason for revising it.

One other point needs to be stressed. Better buses, tubes, trains and taxis will not provide a service superior to that to be had by travelling from door to door in a comfortable car. Improved public transport is, however, the only way to provide accessibility and amenity in places where shops are as piled up as in Oxford Street, where doctors are as thick on the ground as in Harley Street, whose residents live as close together as in

Kensington, where civil servants are so intensely gathered in committees as in Whitehall and so on. Public transport should be given priority in inner London, not because it is morally superior to private cars, which is doubtful, but because activities are so thick on the ground that nothing else will work.

That is not quite true. There is an alternative. It is to reduce drastically the numbers of shops and shoppers in Oxford Street, the number of houses and residents in Kensington and so on. There is even a possibility that this will happen of its own accord over twenty or thirty years, but it has not happened yet on a sufficient scale for it to be possible to dispense with public transport.

Unfortunately, as critics of the ringways are only too aware, making the best use of shared transport is not a possibility that has been given serious consideration. The costs and benefits of building new roads of very modest scale and solely to free hectic high streets and residential neighbourhoods of through traffic while promoting public transport in all possible ways have not yet been explored, least of all by the GLC.

The only public transport improvement tested by the consultants when they were making their traffic forecasts was a megalomaniac engineering project which did not even have the backing of British Rail, whose trains it was intended to benefit. This project was the linking of four of the London main line termini by tunnels that would have come together in a subterranean station under Covent Garden. It never stood the slightest chance of being built and it illustrates the failure of the County Hall planners to understand that a host of unspectacular improvements in quality of service would have been the best way to start pursuing the first of 'the Council's . . . twin objectives of improving public transport in every way . . .'

A start might have been made by restoring buses evicted from old high-street routes by one-way traffic schemes and by placing bus stops at places of greatest convenience to travellers.

When faced with arguments of this sort the authors of the plan have always said that even an upgraded and developed network of bus, train, tube and taxi services, complimented by well arranged interchanges would not stand any hope of arresting the increased use of cars. Yet improvements to public transport services do win new riders.

An example is the first tram-in-a-tunnel or pré-metro services in Brussels. They were started in December 1969 and at the time of the first count in 1970 the number of passengers using the five routes passing through a tunnel under the city centre had picked up 31 per cent in the morning peak, 43 per cent in the evening and 35 per cent at off-peak times, compared with the old days when the trams had had to inch through dense surface traffic.

Market information of this sort is of the utmost importance in discussing the prospects for public transport. Comparisons between, for instance, the £86 million cost of the six and a half mile Fleet line with the £60 million two and a half mile Kensington leg of Ringway 1 are far less helpful. Nevertheless as fuller estimates of the social and financial costs of building motorways through standing neighbourhoods become available, public transport alternatives are likely to look increasingly attractive.

In London's case the motorway system is still sufficiently in its infancy for there to be an opportunity to move towards a transport balance in which greater emphasis is placed on amenity in the streets and measures designed to promote the use of buses, taxis, trains and tubes. Moreover there are signs that after a long sleep the men at 55 Broadway are waking up.

London Transport's abandonment of its long-standing low wages policy for one based on paying better than average rates to compensate for the unconventional working hours of the bus and tubemen is one such sign. Another is the introduction in September 1970 of individual bonuses for bus crews geared to the number of passengers carried. This should lead to revolutionary changes. Passengers may even find that buses stop on being flagged and old ladies may be allowed to hobble aboard without fear.

On the technical side, Route 74 has been fitted with radio telephones. Route 11 is to get an electronic control centre at the Mansion House and London Transport's target is to have 30 per cent of its buses operated by one man by the end of 1971. All this is solid progress. The clearest indication whether or not the pace of improvement is to accelerate will be the energy the GLC puts into bus priorities and into closing busy shopping streets to all traffic except buses in order to improve conditions for people on foot. A big push in this direction would have the twin effects of reducing the amount of road space for cars while up-grading the reliability, speed and convenience of the buses. To the extent that the number of travellers was increased by this approach, London Transport's revenues would be improved and the scope for modernizing the whole service widened.

A complementary policy for bigger car parks at suburban tube and railway stations, new escalators and travelators and covered ways at interchanges, the development of hotels, shopping and office centres above stations and an abandonment of the current no-operating-subsidy policy, would give reasonable assurance of future mobility to inner Londoners.

Travelling in London would not suddenly be paradise but it is very unlikely that Londoners expect such a miracle. As Mrs Ruth Glass showed in her survey of housing in Camden, Londoners are very realistic about what they want and are content with modest improvements.

Out at Harrow, Sutton, Bexleyheath and other places on the fringes of the city, where people are so much less thick on the ground, conditions are different and there is a far better case for building new roads so that cars may be more widely used. Keeping public transport going for those who rely on it will be correspondingly more difficult. Good bus services are likely to continue to such suburban honey pots at Croydon, Kingston, Ilford and Ealing and they will need priorities, as in the inner boroughs. Elsewhere in the outer suburbs residents are likely to find themselves relying increasingly on radio-taxis, and even on radio-mini-buses, to supplement infrequent red bus services.

The contrast between the transport approach put forward for the inner and outer boroughs should serve to underline the fact that there are two Londons. In Victorian London, where the town patterns of a hundred years ago are still dominant and people live close together, public transport will have to be king. Further out in twentieth-century London, amidst the flowering cherries and spacious gardens, there are opportunities for cars to roam.

Far from being a source of regret this prospect of variegated transport in London's contrasting parts should be a source of pleasure. It holds out the prospect of different kinds of places for Londoners to live in and different kinds of transport challenge for the experts. One of the greatest failings of the authors of the plan is that they did not identify these two Londons and face up to the job of designing different transport arrangements for them.

Change, Conservation
and the Tourist Trade
Stephen Mullin

There can be little doubt that the conservation game is proving an increasingly popular pastime for Londoners. The statistics speak for themselves. A fifth of the buildings listed by the Ministry of Housing (now gathered into the Department of the Environment) as being of architectural or historic importance are to be found within the GLC area. Since the Civic Amenities Act of 1967, 164 conservation areas have been designated by the London boroughs, and more are being proposed. In some parts of central London it is rapidly becoming the norm to find oneself in a conservation area: a third of Westminster's land is already controlled in this way; in the adjacent borough of Kensington and Chelsea the proportion is nearer 40 per cent.

Scarcely any building, whatever its age, condition or size, can now be affected by the threat of demolition without someone, somewhere mounting a vigorous campaign for its preservation. Only a few years ago, councillors, property-owners and officials could safely dismiss such protests with a few vague references to 'a handful of cranks': today they have learnt to keep such comments to themselves. If the powerful Ministry of Public Building and Works (now also DOE), outside the law for general planning purposes and bound only by the notorious Circular 100 procedure of 'consultation' with other Ministries, could be brought to its knees over the demolition of New Scotland Yard and associated buildings to the extent of participation in a public inquiry, then clearly no one can consider himself safe from the aggressive conservationist.

It is an extraordinary situation. No other city, at any other time, has simultaneously attempted to re-create the past, preserve the present and plan for a different future. At this moment, considerable sums of money are being expended in an attempt to prolong the life of a group of late seventeenth-century houses in Bloomsbury for a period greater than that of the forty-year leases for which they were originally designed to last. If an inquiry were to be held today on the question of whether Chambers's Somerset House were to be given planning permission, it is extremely likely that a decision would be taken to preserve the jumble of Tudor and Jacobean palaces in the Strand, which it replaced in the eighteenth century.

Of course, very few conservationists would carry this attitude to a logical conclusion, which would amount to declaring the greater part of central London an archaeological museum. The more general viewpoint is best expressed in the words of the GLDP *Report of Studies*: 'Within the fabric, there are many areas with a rich variety of distinctive qualities. Collectively, they form the essence of London's unique character; individually, they provide points of identity and definition.' It is a seductive argument: change, yes, but change which respects the existing scale, maintains the existing usage and preserves the distinctive character of the area.

Moreover, the spectacular growth of London's tourist trade is held up as a solid economic justification for such a policy. Destroy the historic goose, the argument runs, and you eliminate the dollar-earning egg. But the further implications of this line of reasoning are rather disturbing. For this much-prized 'character' depends on the inhabitants and users of a particular area, and their composition is governed by the age, type and size of the buildings available. These in turn are dependent upon land values, which hinge upon the transportation structure and the general pattern of commercial and industrial activity within Greater London as a whole. Freezing one part of this interlocking network means blocking off a whole range of options on the scale of strategic planning, for which the GLC bears overall responsibility.

Conversely, the less that particular activities or styles of living, which it is suggested that the community should preserve or develop, are dependent upon individual, existing buildings or places, the greater the likelihood that London will be able to provide for other objectives of equal importance and increase the diversity of opportunity within the city as a whole. For very often an overt concern for buildings as such masks a general hostility to the processes of change on the part of a particular sectional interest. So, since it has already been raised in public discussion, the tourist industry will be taken as a litmus paper to test out the conservationist case.

It is estimated that at least 75 per cent of overseas visitors to the United Kingdom stay in London at some time during their visit to this country. Assuming that the percentage increase in visitors has remained fairly constant since the last available figures (1968), this would mean that some 5,000,000 foreign visitors will have passed through London in 1970. It is difficult to estimate net earnings from this source, but bearing in mind that foreign currency earnings from tourism in the country as a whole totalled £282 million in 1968, and that this figure is approximately 50 per cent higher than the equivalent sum in 1964, the overall allocation of some £8 million expenditure for staff, maintenance and improvement to London's historic buildings, parks, palaces, museums and art galleries in 1967 would seem a justifiable investment.

But these are the 'national set pieces' to which the GLDP *Report of Studies* refers. And very few tourists come to London specifically to tramp round the National Gallery or visit the Tower of London. Indeed, the British Travel Association's 1969 survey of tourism in London placed Trafalgar Square as London's top attraction, visited by 93 per cent of foreign tourists, while 38 per cent of them described nightclubs, discotheques and trips on the river as among London's most popular amenities. And it is when one looks at shopping centres such as the King's Road and Carnaby Street, or antique markets such as the Portobello Road that the economic justification of the conservationist argument becomes rather more tenuous.

For it is in areas such as these, with their enormous and indisputable attraction to foreign visitors, that the general ambience, character, life – call it what you will – seems to be of equal, if not greater importance than the actual merchandise on sale. The dynamism of such areas is the direct result of rapid and continuous change. The process can be seen as a breaking wave. First, the frothing crest of innovating entrepreneurs with little cash but plenty of ideas. They seize upon an area of decaying buildings under the threat of imminent demolition. Leases are short; rents are low: the surrounding housing is badly in need of improvement and relatively easy to obtain.

The area begins to support new activities and a new community, and this thriving economic base is infiltrated by the solid mass of the wave – people with greater funds and a correspondingly greater degree of caution. Rents begin to rise, and property changes hands at higher and higher prices. Finally the powerful undertow of the wave hauls back the area for profitable re-development by large property-owners. If such a district were to be designated as a conservation area the final undertow of development might be resisted, at least for a time, but the added certainty of usage which it would give would hasten and consolidate stage two of the process and the froth would still move on elsewhere. Such an area might well be an enjoyable place for its new inhabitants, but the life there would no longer be an external phenomenon which outsiders could easily enjoy, but a private affair made possible for the residents by community action.

Actual examples of this process in action can be seen in the boroughs of Islington, Westminster, and Kensington and Chelsea, where conservation areas have already been declared. The Barnsbury area of Islington is a particularly good case in point. Here the middle-class invasion has frozen the pleasant but undistinguished eighteenth- and nineteenth-century street pattern into a make-believe 'village' community. Rising land values and a longer expectation of life for the buildings have led to improvement of the dwellings concerned, causing an exodus of much of the original working-class population. Diversity is *not* encouraged. The Cypriot, West Indian or Mauritian home-owner who paints the exterior of his house in any other colours than cream, white or grey is felt to lower the tone – or, more exactly, the property value – of the neighbourhood. If the town planning committee of the borough has its way, he will soon be unable to paint the brickwork of his house in, say, red or green picked out with white, or indeed in any colour at all. These are matters over which the community apparently feels it should extend its control: here, 'conservation' means a further diminution of the right of the individual to treat his home as a personal toy.

It is possible to maintain a neutral moral stance on such questions, but what is quite clear is that the designation of conservation areas as such will not necessarily 'protect and promote London's diversity of character' (to quote the GLDP *Statement*), nor encourage the formation of dollar-earning tourist-traps. For areas which contain a wide 'demographic spectrum', with a mixture of rich and poor, young and old, families and childless, are inevitably those in a process of change. They are either moving uphill or downhill in monetary value, and the valued 'balanced community' in fact represents an abnormal stage in their evolution, before they settle into an 'imbalanced' but stable state. Public intervention can accelerate the process, but the end result will always be the same.

At the upper-class end of the scale, the buildings themselves become used as symbols to take the place of a vanished physical community. As the corner-shop retreats into the individual deep-freeze and the pavement meeting-place into the private dinner-party, the uniform painting of a Victorian terrace, the restoration of railings to a square and the organization of a tree-planting scheme become methods of demonstrating the common economic and social values of the inhabitants. At the opposite extreme, the poor structural condition of dwellings, their lack of basic amenities and the overcrowding with which this is linked encourage a public life of a sort, and this, coupled with the availability of cheap premises for a wide range of commercial activities, undoubtedly makes them intriguing places for the tourist to visit.

But such conditions can only be maintained, to put it bluntly, by keeping the poor in their place, and whatever the practical effects of the policies of our various political parties it is doubtful whether any of them would publicly endorse this as a positive aim. It is conceivable that an ersatz community of this type could be maintained in the manner of the reconstructed American colonial town of Williamsburg – Petticoat Lane, perhaps, as a kind of human wildlife park, with pearly kings and queens doffing their costumes at the end of each working day before driving home to Dagenham. But such an image would tend to conflict with the picture of London as a great and prosperous city which its inhabitants seem increasingly anxious to project. For it is an unfortunate fact that what the visitor wishes to see and what the host community wants him to see are not by any means the same thing. The classic case is Piccadilly Circus, which in its present state is at once an immense attraction for tourists and a national disgrace in the eyes of a fair proportion of London's inhabitants.

So we are left with the 'transition areas'. In the past, the overall fabric of districts such as that around the Portobello Road has remained in a fairly stable condition: it is the population which has been in transition, with new arrivals to the city using the area as a place to take their breath before moving on to other, more specialized areas. But with the restrictions placed on the growth of London since the war, such areas have proved increasingly hard to find, and so the population has been forced to change the district it already lives in to accommodate its expectations. Either upper-income rehabilitation takes place, or council redevelopment is set in motion. As a result, the central area of London is rapidly closing the cracks in which the young, the unconventional and the newly arrived immigrant were previously able to find a foothold.

All of this may seem some distance from the problems of the tourist industry, or indeed from the destruction or preservation of historic buildings. But in fact this is not the case. What we crudely term 'tourism' is merely a very obvious example of that constant process of sampling and using different ways of living which a city like London should make possible. For example, any study of the present distribution of hotels in the central area will show a close correlation of patterning with designated Conservation Areas. This is no coincidence. The residential hotels of Bayswater, the upper-class enclaves of Mayfair and the conference hotels of Bloomsbury all represent different patterns of living, duration of stay and purpose of visit which have played an active part in consolidating and stabilizing the process of change in these areas. To introduce new hotels of different size, type and purpose will either change the function of the area drastically, or else the limitations of the area itself will cause them to operate inefficiently.

So far, both developers and local authorities have been extraordinarily obtuse over this question. The government incentive scheme, with a straight cash grant per hotel bedroom and no questions asked, has brought a number of inexperienced operators into the market: the scheme's expiry in March 1971 seems to have made them additionally foolhardy. The two main 'hotel boroughs' – Westminster, and Kensington and Chelsea – have allowed their greed for additional rateable value to lead them into bidding against each other for a larger slice of the cake. And the GLC, which as the strategic planning authority has an advisory capacity here, has finally given up the attempt to set up a steering committee to cover the question, after failure to reach agreement with the London Boroughs Association.

Central area hotels of 1,000 bedspaces are now commonly discussed: one proposal for Marble Arch would have room for 1,800. They will not be cheap: steadily rising land values will see to that. Yet the market for which they are designed is apparently that provided by the new 'jumbo jet' package operators, and there will be little money to spare in the pockets of these particular visitors. Furthermore, giant hotels relying on a short stay and a quick turn-round require a large labour force to keep them in operation, and, as has been shown, central London can no longer provide the cheap housing which such a service industry will require.

Then there is the question of what this new type of overseas visitor will actually be doing in London. Two or three days in the city means that every available moment of precious time has to pack the maximum punch of experience. In terms of buildings, this means the large, symbolically expressive monuments. But instant life of the same intensity is no longer to be found in the central area, and time will not be available to explore the subtler rhythms of the area, even supposing that they still exist once one or two of these monsters have come to roost. For the new hotels will have little accommodation except bedrooms, and the first casualties will be small restaurants and shops forced out by developers eager to supply the new mass market.

From any point of view, the sensible areas for provision for this type of visitor are not to be found in the central area but in the latest transition areas to the west and east. Land is cheaper, housing more plentiful, fast public transport routes to the centre already in existence. In addition, the economic boost of a large hotel will add impetus to the breaking wave of change and increase the froth of instant London Life around it. 'Come to colourful Kilburn' may seem a fanciful slogan, but it could well be a reality in a few years time.

Already there are signs that some of the shrewder hotel operators have begun to grasp the advantages of such locations. The proposed redevelopment of St Katherine Dock by the Tower of London has been the most publicized example, but there are also hotels proposed for south of the river, and the European Hotels Consortium (run by five European airlines) has been investigating sites for the cheap end of the market within half an hour's travelling time of the centre. There can be no doubt that the GLC should actively encourage such proposals and restrain the demands of the richer inner London boroughs with all the means at its disposal – which, regrettably, are slender enough. For the logical sites for such new hotels are along the new rapid transit routes of the Victoria line and the Fleet line which run through the depressed areas of the East End and north-west and north-east London. New development of this nature is a natural lever for assisting the economic recovery of these areas.

But the jumbo-jet tourist is not the only new factor on the scene. For the past few years the number of overseas visitors coming for purposes other than 'tourism' has been steadily increasing. In 1968 20 per cent came on business, 18 per cent to visit friends and relatives, 2 per cent to study and a further 15 per cent for 'other' reasons. Unike the traditional tourist, this sector is not restricted to the summer holiday season, and it has probably been responsible for the dramatic expansion of the season in recent years. Nor are these broad categories a reliable guide to the actual purpose of visit, for rising standards of living and increasing ease of travel now allow individuals to extend their normal patterns of living into the international sphere.

An American professor, for example, may travel to London with his family to do a month's research at the British Museum en route for a holiday in Europe. While there, he may look up old friends, attend a conference, give a couple of seminars and exchange ideas with colleagues, as well as enjoying the stimulus of familiar activities carried out in a new and exotic setting. In short, he will be a multi-purpose transient, and the fact that he was not born in this country makes him no different from British citizens who are increasingly making use of their capital for periods of relatively short duration for exactly the same reasons.

But at the moment almost no provision is made for this kind of visitor. His average length of stay – thirty-four days – is far too long for most central hotels, especially during the summer. And in any case the type of accommodation he requires, and the facilities he needs, are not those which they can generally supply. He will probably require easy access to university institutions, specialist libraries or head offices of businesses, all of which tend to be located in the central area. He may need space for study or informal conferences. And he will almost certainly wish to explore the more private life of the capital, and live for a while as a Londoner.

The central area also contains the largest proportion of London's older buildings. Most of them are domestic in scale, for London is still an intimate city and this is one of its attractions for visitors. Their pleasures too are small-scale: they do not register well from the windows of a charter coach and they need living in to bring out their flavour. Unless they contain features of unique significance their chances of survival are slim. Many of them owe their continued existence to a quirk of location which has left them in a low-value backwater isolated from the tide of redevelopment: they may well have been requisitioned during the war for temporary accommodation and be overcrowded as a result. In either case their structural condition is likely to be poor, and, if they are still in use as housing, they usually do not comply with public health standards.

Their rehabilitation presents enormous difficulties at the moment. Ensuring their survival for a period of sixty years life as housing, if not impossible, may well involve a borough or private estate with severe problems of housing finance already in considerable expenditure for little return. Subdivision into smaller units may mean the obliteration of most of their attractive internal features – panelling, plasterwork, large rooms. If the ground floors are occupied by shops, then the cobbler, the greengrocer and the newsagent may have to move in order that a more profitable tenant may subsidize the work required. And in any case the original inhabitants may have no particular wish to stay there if the alternative is a modern flat near by.

So the prospect is that of the preservation of a few isolated building specimens, like butterflies in a case, possibly backed up by the husks of a number of others – gutted to provide inconvenient and sub-standard office space – and a range of fancy infill in coy pastiche. Better the bulldozer. But there is an alternative. The relatively short potential life of these buildings could be turned to advantage. For most of the large institutions in the central area – university buildings, the hospitals, the British Museum Library, even large office blocks – also have a relatively short life ahead of them, whatever their structural condition. Already the problems of housing and travelling in the congested centre are hitting staff and users hard, and any expansion is well-nigh impossible. Dispersal will inevitably come – sooner, rather than later, if the GLC were to take the logical step of reducing rather than increasing accessibility to the centre and letting it bleed gracefully to death. But a great deal of public capital is tied up in these buildings, and the best use must be made of it in the meantime.

New, long-lived buildings such as student hostels will only compound the problem, and in any case it is generally realized at long last that they represent a supremely unsatisfactory solution to this particular area of housing need. But the older eighteenth-

and nineteenth-century buildings in the area offer ideal opportunities for conversion into short-stay market-price accommodation with facilities for formal and informal meetings, private study, computer information terminals and fly-by-night pundits. There would be no need to restrict such accommodation to overseas visitors, nor to particular categories of use. The only criteria would be the duration of stay and the specialized requirements of the visitor: classifications such as 'student', 'businessman' and 'academic' would be as irrelevant as the range of accommodation would be varied.

Such short-term test-beds would allow the GLC an unrivalled opportunity for experimentation. Peter Cowan's recent suggestion that central area office activity could revert to a loosely organized coffee-house network of top-grade executives could be explored immediately: the experience gained could be applied to extending the variety and range of living accommodation in London, so rigidly corseted by outdated user categories at the moment. The GLC could justifiably call upon government funds for assistance, as the city of Delft has done for a similar project, and it already has to hand an ideal area to start with in the shape of the Covent Garden district, for which it now has overall responsibility. Most important of all, perhaps, the buildings concerned would not be suffered as a kind of aesthetic albatross, but used for a purpose for which they are eminently suited and enjoyed to the hilt before they finally fall apart at the seams. Furthermore, the GLC is eminently suited to undertake such action, in its role as strategic planning authority. For while the boroughs are receptive enough to the idea of conservation, through pressure from well-heeled minority groups, this amounts to no more than the consolidation and promotion of existing styles of living. If London is not to stagnate, it needs a countervailing force to promote innovation and change both for the voiceless and underprivileged and for the prosperous and sophisticated transient of the immediate future. The examples discussed are only a fragment of the total range of opportunity, but they do give a key to the potential role of the GLC.

For in a very real sense we are, increasingly, all of us tourists;

and in a constantly accelerating environment of change every building, no matter how recent, is a historic one. Whether we exploit those buildings to their full potential, or allow them to constrict our lives instead, may mark the difference between London as a capital of global significance and as a sleepy European backwater.

The City Scene   Sylvia and Sam Webb

Although it is impossible at present to foresee all the developments that are to affect the physical shape and character of London in the twenty-first century, certain trends in the new large-scale renewal building projects are already very apparent, and it is all too likely that London will slowly emerge as a replica of any second-rate American city.

Before the office ban of 1964, the London newspapers almost every evening carried stories of bigger and better office blocks that had received planning permission, and this coupled with the Government's policy to allow the private motorist unlimited freedom of access to every part of London have produced the skyscraper-type building and wider roads which have so radically changed London's character and shape.

It was thought that the 1964 office ban would no longer make it easy for men to play real-life monopoly with building projects. But now the accent is on hotels, spurred on by the Labour Government's grant to the developer of £1,000 per bedroom. Every evening the city's newspapers now boast photographs of proposed skyscraper hotels, but as these buildings rise from their muddy sites, will they destroy the London that the tourist has come to see?

Now that the 600 ft height barrier has been burst by Mr Richard Seifert's National Westminster Bank building, how long will we have to wait for the next jump up to 900 or 1,000 ft?

If New York in the pre-Great War era is any guide, the great leap forward will not be long in coming. There the 612 ft Singer building was overhauled before its tenants had time to settle in by the 715 ft Metropolitan Life Assurance building. Excessive cost of the land in Manhattan was the main reason for building so high and while these buildings were under construction, others, like the Equitable Life Assurance rising to 909 ft, were already

on architects' drawing boards. In London, only the office ban
has prevented massive investment into office buildings recently,
but political pressures at present being brought to bear may
shortly lift this ban, and it is likely that as more and more high
buildings rise within the next ten or fifteen years St Paul's will be
reduced in scale to that of the church at the top of Wall Street.

In *The Property Boom*, Oliver Marriot stated that the old LCC
formula of trading land from a developer's site for road widening,
by transferring the plot ratio from the traded land to the remaining land, had fallen badly into disrepute, possibly because giant
buildings emerged in unsuitable places and produced not only
visual conflicts but physical problems, with new stress points on
the public transport system.

However, this trading policy to facilitate road widening is still
in operation despite the Greater London Development Plan:

Areas over which high plot ratios are allowed should be relatively
small and the traffic arrangements should be particularly good. In
rare cases in Central London where a site is of outstanding importance a higher plot ratio may occasionally be justified provided that
transport facilities, access and other conditions make it specifically
appropriate [para. 13.9].

Any attempts the GLC may make to stop the rash of high buildings in the wrong places by their high buildings policy will
therefore be nullified by their massive road proposals for central
London.

London, at present, lies innocent and unsuspecting, like a
latter-day Paris, victim of the Schlieffen Plan of road widening
of the GLC and the Department of the Environment. For all
the brave talk, central London could well be destroyed by the
massive roads that point at its heart and the gigantic buildings
that will rise at almost every major road junction.

What sort of London will this brave new plan bring us?
Already we have the moonscape of Westway, sweeping past the
slums of Acklam Road and on through brand-new housing estates
just recently completed and luckily modified to reduce the noise
by the same GLC that produced the road. Three times a minute at
rush hours, commuter trains thunder past the twenty-three-acre

domino-patterned Doddington Road Estate in Wandsworth with
its 900 homes, shattering the ear drums, as the sound waves blast
back and forth from block to block.

As commercial developments have got bigger, so have housing
estates built by local authorities. In September 1970, the *Architectural Review* rated the Aylesbury Estate at Southwark a place in
the *Guinness Book of Records* as

the longest system built housing block in Europe, the largest housing
project ever undertaken by a London borough, the most comprehensive upper-level deck system in the country, and the largest use of
'12M Jespersen' on one site. . . . The tenants, 2000 in number, are
unlikely to forget or to forgive the lack of private open space, the
monotony and the regimentation of their estate writ large.

The collapse of Ronan Point brought with it the end of subsidies for high tower blocks. Already some architects had begun
to rebel against tower blocks, together with sociologists, newspapers and, most important, the tenants. Many of these blocks
need ever have been built if it hadn't been for the advent of the
tower crane and Ministry subsidies? The simple answer to Ronan
Point is 'no'. For when some tenants objected to being housed in
tower blocks after the collapse, Newham's Town Clerk issued the
following statement : 'I would point out that the density of the
flats, taken in relation to the surrounding land, is much lower
than the density of the houses they replace . . .' The Ronan Point
site of two-storey bye-law houses could quite easily have been
replaced by five-storey terraces housing more people, the top two
floors with a garden on the roof, the next two with a garden on
the ground and the real ground floor garaging cars. The change in
emphasis in subsidies has led naturally from the tallest system
building in the world to the longest.

The reason for the local authorities developing larger and
larger sites into one-class one-use future ghettoes is not difficult to
understand. The bigger the site, the greater the money the Ministry allows, and the easier it is to mitigate the high cost of land.
But it is in the inner London boroughs that land costs become
really acute and the rents of the housing developed grow out of
proportion to the ability of people to pay for them. Some of these

boroughs must soon charge an economic rent if the new housing is not to become an enormous drain on their resources. But whether people will pay £20 per week for a house they will never own is open to question. This factor, plus the rising cost of land, the enormous 83 per cent burden of interest payable by the local authority on the money loaned for housing, will stop the building of housing in central London for all but the very rich. Not many people realize that the capital cost of local authority housing represents only 17 per cent of the total cost, the remainder being spent on interest on the money loaned. 'Perhaps fifty years from now school children will wonder why a civilized society has tolerated such a system for so long,' Ruth Glass said in her Report, *Housing in Camden*.

As the amount of rentable accommodation gets smaller and smaller in central London, the furnished and decontrolled unfurnished tenants become like rabbits trapped in the centre of a cornfield as the reaper gets nearer. The loss of privately rented accommodation is enormous as these areas are redeveloped. In 1914, 90 per cent of all housing in Great Britain was rented from private landlords. By 1947, 61 per cent, 1961, 31 per cent and by 1967, 23 per cent.

London could be well on the way to creating a new urban poor, alienated, badly educated, socially deprived and appallingly housed. All the boroughs have enormous housing lists, many people have been on them and died on them, some since 1945, without enough money to save up for a deposit on a house, let alone the wage packet to qualify for a mortgage. The slums of London will not disappear, people will slowly spill over into the semis of the thirties in places like West Hendon, East Finchley, Kingsbury and Wembley. This is the most serious problem in London today and for the future.

The rich trend-setters of the last half of the nineteenth century commuted vast distances to work in London. It was a status symbol to live in Brighton and travel into the new terminus at Victoria. This is a life-style now adopted by many thousands of people today as they travel in from north Kent, Dover, Folkestone, Hastings, Bexhill, Eastbourne and Brighton. Pressures of

living, the choice of a decent sized house, good schools and recrea-
tional facilities have driven the middle classes in desperation to
escape from a situation that is beyond their comprehension. A new
situation will develop with the advent of the advanced passenger train travelling at speeds up to 150 m.p.h. Stations will have
to be an hour apart to attain these speeds and it will be possible
to live in the Peak District or along the Welsh border country in
a bijou farm labourer's cottage, drive to the nearest main-line
station and hurtle into central London in the time it takes people
to travel in from Edgware or Ongar. Unless the fares are astro-
nomically high, the choice will be opened to the more highly
skilled in this 150-mile belt to forgo an hour's sleep in the morning for a higher salary and advanced status amongst the neighbours. So London would draw in its managerial, executive and
professional classes from cities as far away as Manchester. The
effect in the rating system would be catastrophic, and reflect the
trend that has been set up in North-American cities. New York
City has become so desperate that sites are rated on the maximum
sized property that could theoretically be developed. Famous
buildings of architectural merit like the Lever Building could
well be doomed to demolition and replaced with buildings rising
sheer from the pavement for hundreds of feet, using up every
available square inch of the ground upon which they stand. Why
should London be so different?

But there are some hopeful signs as people are brought back
into the centre of London. Slowly the Barbican buildings have
risen from the ground. St Katharine Dock is to see new life, so
is the Foundling Estate in Bloomsbury with its stepped terraces
of flats and shops underneath. Each of these is a mixed development of housing, commerce and shops carried out with a verve
and panache that Brunel might have envied. The local authorities
are not always so fortunate, however, when it comes to multi-use
of sites and often their developments reflect their antiquated
bureaucratic administrative system.

Mixed development is not a new phenomenon to London,
indeed the whole of the London building fabric was once a
higgeldy-piggeldy mixture of factories, banks, offices, worshops,

schools, churches, stores, markets and homes for clergymen, working families, gentlefolk, apprentices, articled clerks and aristocrats. The pattern for zoning London emerged during the thirties and was consolidated by Lord Silkin's Town and Country Planning Act of 1947 and its subsequent numerous revisions and amendments. Single-use buildings have emerged all over London because of it, the only concessions being made for the lower two floors of a successful shopping area. It might seem obvious to the layman that an area which needed housing, welfare facilities, a health centre, shops and library and community facilities could have them all under one roof sharing foundations, drainage, boiler plant, parking, lifts, etc. If the site is small and land costs high, it would seem self-evident. But the Ministries themselves have failed to grasp this opportunity. To minds bludgeoned by in and out trays, terms of reference and Ministry circulars, such coordination is anathema. Far, far better for the administrator, if all users are on different pieces of land where it is possible to allocate the total cost of the one-use building. Enormous obstacles are thrown in the path of any architect who is foolhardy enough to try. Money for the various uses would have to be sanctioned by, for example, the Departments of the Environment, Health and Education and even they could all change their titles in the course of one job, witness recent events, before they have argued out the percentage costs of the services, structure and foundations and planting between them. Small wonder that the giant Doddington Scheme provides its shop, pub, social centre, day centre, clinic and library in single- or two-storey brick buildings, away from the stark uncompromising cliffs of housing. It all seems so pointless when all the loans are sanctioned by the Treasury and the money comes out of the taxpayer's pockets anyway.

When the housing-cost yardstick was introduced, it was not at first realized what a powerful weapon it could be in the hands of a government for savings in the public sector. Complex tables like PAYE forms relating to density, average occupancy rates and bedspace density fixed the amount a scheme would cost at the planning stage. In theory, it was very laudable, in practice it has proved much the reverse. Prices of materials, wages and interest rates have risen so fast that the Government dropped full central heating from the Parker Morris recommendations, and the fixed sums allocated meant that standards and materials used dropped too. When a building is being paid for over sixty years and some of the materials have a useful life of only twenty years, then maintenance costs are bound to be high. Yet the Ministry of Housing has never taken maintenance into account. The implications of this can be seen most clearly at Coventry, almost entirely rebuilt since the war, where the housing department spends as much on the maintenance of its postwar buildings as it does on the repayment of the loans that finance their construction. The picture must be much the same for the GLC and the London boroughs. Such an attitude could in the end force them to drop their housing targets, as they fight hard to stop their postwar housing becoming as bad as the slums they have replaced.

Cooperation between potential neighbours and owners of sites has disappeared as land and property values have soared. The shrewd property developer wants his slice of the city cake just as clearly defined and uncomplicated as the local authority. As it is now unlikely that large investors in property can be persuaded and the local authorities do not at present have the power to buy up and develop land for profit, is there a way of getting mixed development? As things stand, as well as being expensive, council housing is undesirable socially, in that more often than not, the occupants want to rebel as they are tagged and labelled by the monotony of their and their neighbours' identical accommodation. While still unable to purchase their own homes, many families would be ready to contribute not only to the styling of the interior of their house to make it as they want, but would also like to be able to pay for additional extras such as floor-to-ceiling glazing, a large sun terrace or balcony, a larger or extra living room or full central heating. This social desire, together with the developers' desire to make a profit, could be harnessed by cooperation between the local authority and the private developer and brought to mutual fruition.

Carcass structures to take mixed uses could be designed and

constructed with minimal services and let in the same way as a developer now leases a shop or store, as a shell. The developer could then negotiate with prospective tenants for the commercial lettings, and the local authority could advertise for do-it-yourself home-makers, who would come forward from many social groupings. Many men and women would literally carry out this finishing work themselves, using their own preferred materials and colour schemes so that the end result would be multi-coloured individually shaped dwellings. Although it could be argued that the end result could be a cacophony of self-expression, its impact could not possibly be as psychologically disturbing as that of the concrete filing cabinets that have been devised as homes.

Large areas of land exist ripe for experiments of this kind – railways used and disused and the docklands and basins of east London. If despite the Roskill Commission's majority verdict, Foulness does become London's third airport, then this would be an opportunity to free the land lining the Thames at present occupied by the docks. Foulness could then be developed as a sea port and the dock area for the whole of London and its hinterland. Container ships could off-load, goods could be transferred to barges and carried up the Thames to London and beyond. If money was invested into widening the existing canals the goods could be carried right up into Birmingham without going by road at all. In addition the barrier now proposed could incorporate a road bridge to link to north Kent and the Channel Tunnel. Vehicles coming from Europe could then travel straight up the east coast to Hull and north east of England without passing through London. Such a move could have the effect of introducing capital investment into the rundown areas of east London. A glimpse of London 2000?

When Hillaire Belloc wrote of his 'two acres of land just south of the Strand' he was hardly thinking of the vast area of south London which is so near to the City and West End and Westminster, and yet so poorly developed. Today it is peopled by the cultural elite and the office workers, transient homes for precious pictures viewed in awed respect in the concrete pile of the Hayward Gallery. It is hard to believe that millions of people enjoyed themselves here at the Festival of Britain in the far-off summer of 1951. It stands today as a mute example of a fitting epitaph to the neat zoning on a planner's map.

How could new life be injected into this area? Imagine instead Charing Cross Station removed from its site in the Strand and combined with Waterloo. Here morning commuters would step off trains and be carried up from the central concourse by escalators to travelators running into the West End on the other side of the river over a new bridge. The travelators crossing the bridge could be encased in glass providing views of the Houses of Parliament, the Thames and the City beyond. On the bridge would be shops, cafés and restaurants, some large, some small, and above the bridge a supporting structure could house offices and homes for thousands of people. This vast generator would encourage investment in the South Bank, the revenue for renting accommodation would accrue to British Rail and during the day thousands of inquisitive visitors and tourists would come lured by its mysterious delights, to travel up in its inclined lifts and view the city and explore the high level shops and restaurants. This 'London Link' is not beyond reach and could be built today.

Major transportation problems have to be tackled if we are to liberate London from its massive road widening proposals. One of the ways could be by the development and construction of 'route buildings'. Regent's Park terraces, Regent Street, the Georgian terraces and squares of London are all continuous buildings, they provide a fabric of infinite variety and yet they lack only one element that the modern route building would provide – movement. In the form of large steel structures route buildings could be designed to support local roads, buses and moving pavements as well as providing a continuous covered shopping arcade at above ground level. The route building, because of its linear growth pattern, could accommodate continuous car parking lots below ground, and below these the main supply pipe lines for sewers, telephones, electrical, water and gas services, and also postal and freight tunnels which would service not only the route building but the developments it passes through. The structure would need to be of bridge-building proportions to support mass transport systems. It would be sensible therefore to exploit the necessary continuity of its shape by constructing it of sufficient strength and height to support offices and homes above the street and shopping arcade. These homes and offices would take the form of individually shaped and constructed lightweight prefabricated units that would sit on, and be strapped to, the structure. Local 'sky streets' could be established at the higher levels serving this accommodation, and these streets could in places extend themselves as bridges to the existing surrounding buildings thus producing upper circulation routes.

The structure at its base could have large building of different shapes and uses grafted onto it. Theatres and department stores would thrive as shoppers and passers-by were introduced to their displays and advertisements at ground and gallery levels.

The route building would in itself be a generator of life and activity and could be adaptable and flexible as site conditions change. In parts it could rise crammed to capacity, in other sections it could merely be a viaduct carrying the road, mass transport systems and mechanical services.

The skilful designer of new developments could design accommodation to allow the sun's rays to be enjoyed at ground level. Basement accommodation, though expensive to provide, should, if necessary, be imposed on developers (in the same way as height restrictions above ground) so that all ancillary accommodation not requiring natural light is placed underground and not allowed to consume sky space. Also the new development can be designed to step back in places to contain terraces in the air, protected from the wind and yet producing open space. Roof space as such should not exist. Every roof should be developed as a terrace with horizontal or ramped connection to surrounding terraces. (In New York the Port Authority is extraordinarily building the World Trade Centre which consists of twin identical towers, higher than the Empire State Building, immediately alongside one another without a single connection at the upper levels.) The designer should also recognize the appalling street conditions produced for pedestrians in the wind vortices from tower buildings, and try to overcome this discomfort with arcades or wind-break landscaping.

Every year some thousands of people despair of London, give up and move out, while council leaders of the London boroughs despair of solving their housing problems. For a city to remain alive physically and economically, a balance must be struck so that the people who work and live there lead reasonably pleasant lives. Successive Governments have relied on cheap labour to keep London's essential services moving. When it became difficult to get staff, London Transport encouraged West Indians to come and drive buses and trains. The same happened to the hospitals. Just as the Australians have congregated in Earls Court so the immigrant West Indian, Indian or Pakistani has tended to con-gregate in specific areas, no doubt made worse by the unwritten laws of estate agents and property values. These are the people who will be left behind through no fault of their own, while others who can afford to move out. The people most necessary for the city, and who need to live there, are most often the most expendable on the housing market. Everyone should have a choice of places to work, homes, schools, shops and transport. Without this choice the city becomes a place in which one spends one's life fighting for survival.

As cities become vast commercial jungles, unbearable to move in, necessary to work in, impossible to live in, some pundits project a future in which cities will become obsolete. The indi-vidual will be free to move from place to place encapsulated in an air-conditioned, pre-programmed living vehicle (a kind of sophisticated de-luxe caravan) and all his communication with others and his work schedules will be transacted with audio-visual aids.

If, and when, this state of limbo is ever realized, society will cease to exist as we know it today. And whereas anarchists may delight and philosophize on the freedom to come, it is possible that this dispersal of people into independent units will be a bad thing. Cities are generators of talent, commerce and wealth. Whilst cities exist, man will remain competitive, aware of his fellow workers and their pursuit of knowledge and the unknown.

Also he is able to see his work as it is reflected in the fields of others. If dispersal of people is inevitable in the specialization of working activities, zoning, together with the isolation it produces, can only result in a monomania of social inbreeding. It is not the concept of the city that is at fault. It is society's natural reaction to abandon it as a machine which is at present destroying itself and the individual in the process.

The Future London   Peter Hall

Totally lacking in the Greater London Development Plan is any sense of a grand design. The GLC planners would have a ready justification: they are trying, they would say, to escape from the old tyranny of the rigid master plan, which specified every square foot of land use, and which was often as not out of date long before Whitehall set its stamp of approval on it. But in trying to keep his options open to suit changing circumstances in a dynamic city, the planner may fall into the opposite trap: of failing to provide any proposals the people can grasp at all. True, the GLDP is a broad strategic plan. But such a plan should start by identifying the main features of the way London works now, the main ways in which these are unsatisfactory according to certain defined criteria of performance, and the main ways in which improvements could come about. It should be, to borrow the new terminology, truly a *structure* plan: a plan which systematically analyses the relationships between patterns of physical structures and patterns of activities, and which seeks to make improvements in the first so as to bring about desirable changes in the second.

To do this, any London plan must start by recognizing that the future London will grow out of the present London, and is in large measure fixed by it. That is true even over the longest of historical terms: roads built by Roman legionaries twenty centuries ago still serve as London's main traffic arteries, the financial centre still clusters round the site of a bridge built around the year 300, desirable residential areas (and now hotels) spread west of the centre to avoid smoke pollution of a bygone age. And in the short and medium term – broadly, up to thirty or forty years from 1970 – the influence of the present London will be all-persuasive. The important problem is to identify precisely what freedom of choice it offers.

The present structure

For this purpose of analysis, London may be cut up schematically into broad zones. At the centre, within an astonishingly small area bounded by the main railway stations, there is the greatest concentration of workers, every weekday, to be found in Europe. Less than a quarter of a million people sleep here at night, over a million and a quarter work here during the day. They include most of the richest of London's workers – the professionals and the managers in finance, in publishing, in advertising, in government – and a surprising proportion of the poorest: the barmaids and the waiters, the refuse collectors and the cloakroom attendants who keep the great concentration of service industries going. Furthermore, in this central concentration of jobs the richest and the poorest seem to be growing at the expense of the middle: there are more and more advertising executives each year, more and more chambermaids in the new hotels, but fewer and fewer routine office workers in the very centre.

The great majority of these central workers commute in from outside the central area, and an appreciable minority – well over two hundred thousand – travel long distances, fifteen miles or more. Three quarters of them come by train for all or part of their journey. The richest among the work force tend either to travel long distances from outer suburban or rural retreats, or to live very close. The middle live appropriately at middle distances, though some of the younger among them are being driven out increasing distances to find homes they can afford. The poor, paradoxically, live very close to their work.

It is paradoxical, because their homes stand on expensive land. It is doubly paradoxical, because many of them pay higher rents than the rich: higher, that is, in terms of the space they occupy. They compete for space, in the privately rented sector, with a vast and shifting army of people better able to pay. The West Indian bus driver and the Irish barman compete for a private flat with the group of students living on grants, with the band of young secretaries, with older people who have decided to move back into town because their children have grown up, with playboy bachelors. The reasons why they are involved in this paradox are simple. They earn too little to afford to buy their own houses. They may have been here too short a time, or be otherwise disqualified, to compete for a council flat. They have limited knowledge of housing possibilities at greater distances from the centre. If they work early or late, as many do, public transport becomes a problem.

Consequently, the inner ring of London – the ring just outside the central area, and forming an irregular band three to four miles wide around it – is an area of contrasts. In it live many of the richest people in London, and many of the poorest. They all live at relatively high densities compared with other Londoners, many of them – even the rich – in flats rather than houses. Car ownership is generally lower than elsewhere, and not just because of poverty; owning a car here is more troublesome than elsewhere, and tubes and taxis make it less essential. Though there is obvious segregation in this ring – more of the poor live east and south, more of the rich live west and north – in many areas the two groups live cheek by jowl. Perhaps this is less evident than it was: for as whole streets are improved, as the house agents put it, the rich social mixture characteristic of the old London disappears. But it is still evident in Kensington and in Camden Town, in Islington and in Peckham.

This inner zone is mainly a zone of homes. But it also contains a surprising number of jobs. Surprising, because so many of them are tucked away in small workshops, in mews and back yards, or in a host of localized service industries like shops and repair workshops. The inner zone is a great seedbed for bright entrepreneurs with little capital but plenty of ideas: the laboratory assistant who breaks away to manufacture his own scientific equipment for the big hospitals, the art-school graduate who makes a success out of freaky lighting. It is also a home of lost industrial causes: the small tailor's or carpenter's shop which ticks over, just making a living, in aged and often run-down premises, while more thrusting competitors move out to modern factories in new towns. Lastly, it also houses vast areas developed in Victorian times for docks and railway yards, not all of which are by any means obviously needed today.

Surrounding it is an outer zone, developed with extraordinary speed between the two world wars. To the stranger it appears like an endless suburban sea. Only the resident develops a strong sense of locality that makes Harrow a distinct place from Wembley, Bromley quite different from Bexley. Here, many of the residents bought their homes when both were young, forty years ago; now the children have grown up and moved away, and the population is falling. Those still at work may commute by tube or Southern Electric to central area offices and shops. But many others work in local factories or shops, making short commuter journeys which are not well served by public transport; far more commonly than central area commuters, they tend to use their own cars. Many work in big industrial concentrations developed in the 1920s and 1930s, such as the Great West Road, Park Royal or the Lea Valley. There, they are joined by a host of slightly longer-distance commuters who have come, also by car for the most part, from just across the Green Belt. The result may be acute local traffic congestion at the rush hours. Heathrow Airport, one of the biggest concentrations of employment in outer London has very much the same pattern.

The outer boundary of this last zone is also, very roughly, the boundary of the area of the Greater London Council. Beyond that is the Green Belt (which is partly within the GLC area) and beyond that the fast-growing ring of towns and villages, up to forty miles from central London, which the planners term the outer metropolitan area. Nearly all these planners would agree that in some important sense all or part of this area has functional relationships with London, and should properly be planned with it. But they would differ very much on the precise details of definition. Meanwhile, the GLC boundary appears fairly immutable. Even the 1969 report of the Redcliffe-Maud commission on local government in England, in a proposed holocaust of boundaries, did not propose any change in it.

Some problems: jobs, housing, transport

From this deliberately crude sketch, it is already possible to identify most of the main problems that now plague London. Most of them can be summed up in the one word that London is most short of : space. But shortage of space means different things in different places.

In the centre, the problem is the continued growth of some sorts of jobs, and the resulting competition for land. The office boom is succeeded by the hotel boom; both activities are essentially central area activities, though the hotel boom threatens to give central London a new definition, taking its western boundary out to Hammersmith and Shepherd's Bush by 1980. In itself, it might be thought that growth of jobs is no problem; after all, that is what quite a large part of Britain, aided by the Government, is trying without much success to achieve. And indeed, the GLDP itself views the process in less alarmist a light than ever the old LCC did. At any rate, it is good for the GLC's finances; for it increases the volume of highly rated commercial premises. On the other hand, it might be argued, the market will sort out the problem of competition for land, driving out those needing less to be at the centre, perhaps to locations in the suburbs or outer metropolitan area, perhaps out of London altogether. The trouble of course is that it does not work like that; instead of displacing older commercial activities, new commercial activities tend to displace homes. The offices did that twenty years ago in Bloomsbury and Mayfair; now the hotels threaten to do it, in Earls Court and Shepherd's Bush.

At the same time, there are grave implications for transport. As will be explained in a moment, London's residential population is dropping. An increasing number of central jobs will need to be manned by a decreasing labour force – a ludicrous situation, and one unlikely to be solved by greater productivity. (You do not readily automate advertising copywriters or hotel room service.) Therefore, the shortage can be met only by cramming more people into London to live, or by providing for more people to travel ever longer commuting distances beyond the Green Belt.

(Or – but no one seriously considers the possibility – nibbling at the Green Belt itself.) The trouble is that though the GLC now has responsibility for London Transport, it has no such responsibility for British Rail, which is the main provider of long-distance commuter transport. Many, though not all, of their services are overloaded, and the bill for capital improvements will go to the central government.

There is one logical way out of this impasse. It is to restrict the total amount of employment in London by planning controls, or some sort of financial disincentive (such as a payroll tax), or both; and then to leave competition to sort out those best qualified to stay. Routine office jobs could be encouraged to move even more rapidly than they have up to now – the Location of Offices Bureau has been moving an average of 10,000 a year – by encouraging (rather than restricting, as now) office construction in the outer metropolitan area, which is as far as most offices are willing to move. Factories occupying old premises, too, could be encouraged to go. If a life could be put on planning permissions in non-purpose-built structures – houses converted into offices or Methodist churches converted into factories – that would eventually encourage the process, thus making more room for the expansion that will come. And the central Government could use more leverage, both on its own routine activities and on other sectors where its investment policies are critical. The continued growth of the University of London on some of the most valuable land in the metropolis, which necessitates very expensive building programmes which could be carried out at a fraction of the cost elsewhere, and which exacerbates the housing problem through the presence of thousands of students, is one of the least comprehensible facets of postwar London. Yet far from actively encouraging its removal, local authorities are compounding the error by the construction of new polytechnics.

The trouble is that here as elsewhere, the local authorities speak with two voices. The Inner London Education Authority, and the education committees of the outer boroughs are certainly not responsible to the GLC planners on polytechnic construction. (Yet what sort of structure plan is it that has no real control

over an explosively growing activity like polytechnic education?)
Worse, the GLC's own financial position gives it a built-in incentive to encourage as much activity of every sort to stay in
London as possible. Offices, shops, factories, even the tattiest
workshop still contribute to the rates. And at a time when the
domestic rateable contribution is going down, that is no small
matter.

This problem is most nicely illustrated in the inner boroughs.
Here, the population is falling due to slum-clearance schemes
and the rehabilitation of old houses by middle-class families,
which replaces several families by one. The new housing schemes
which replace the old slums are justly attacked by social planners
for their high-density inhumanity, notwithstanding the fact that
the densities are lower than those of the old slums. Supporters of
the Town and Country Planning Association will point out that
the process also involves the general taxpayer, and the London
ratepayer, in enormous subsidy contributions; they are not slow
to quote in support Dr Peter Stone, now a senior GLC planner,
whose eleven-year-old research showed conclusively that low-
density solutions were economically better for the whole community. Yet if densities were lowered to the point that no one
need live off the ground, the available work force to man the
critical low-paid service industries would drop still more
catastrophically. Gaps between buses would grow still bigger, it
would take longer to get a sandwich in the pub at lunchtime, and
the central London economy would be even more strained. So in
the plan, the GLC fails to give the boroughs any clear guidelines
at all on the critical question of densities. Each borough will be
free to build to the point that its ratepayers, or central Government, cries halt.

Some relief might be found in the outer boroughs. It will not
be dramatic; after all, few areas in those boroughs were developed
more than fifty years ago; and much of the housing will be good
for some decades yet. But here and there, pockets of older housing,
or even of younger housing built at very low densities, coupled
with waste land, could hopefully be redeveloped, to give a useful
bonus in extra homes. The trouble, as the GLC soon found, is

that the boroughs intend to be masters in their own house. Here
as elsewhere, the GLC is an authority with colossal paper responsibilities, and precious few detailed powers.

Overlying all these problems, and in a sense binding them together, is the general controversy about transport. The GLC has
been subject to many silly and ill-informed criticisms on this
score, but certain good ones still remain. Admitting the enormous
increase in private car traffic that is almost certain to arise, whatever constraints and whatever the variation in basic parameters
like car ownership, it still remains a valid point that the GLC
plans never considered the transport proposals in terms of alternative patterns for the future London; that rail proposals were
introduced only belatedly, at the last stage; and that no firm
method of testing the value of rail plans, as against road plans,
has yet been devised for the purpose of fixing priorities. The most
basic of these questions, undoubtedly, is the lack of any alternative activity patterns. In an age when every planning textbook
calls for evaluation of alternative plans as standard practice, the
GLDP has none. Though there are alternative transport plans in
plenty, all are judged in relation to a single vision of the future
London.

The GLC's one excuse is the one already quoted at the beginning of this chapter: that the future London is in large measure
fixed by the present London. But really, this will not do; for it
does not alter the fact that the future must hold alternative possibilities, whose consequences need to be explored. *Tomorrow's
London*, indeed, does begin to explore them in a tentative way.
It discusses the implications for population density level of a rich
man's London and a poor man's London, for instance. But the
whole process needs taking much further.

Policy alternatives for the future

First, there are alternative patterns of activities and job. Central
London could contain less jobs or more. (The residue, squeezed
out, could go to other places in London, or outside.) Within
central London, the jobs, now scattered, could be more concen-

trated to make them more accessible to transport. (They could hardly be more scattered than at present.) Existing office rights on old converted houses, in places like Bloomsbury and Belgravia, could be traded in for new rights near the terminal railway stations and near existing or planned tube lines. The major strategic centres proposed in the GLDP, at suburban distances of about ten miles from the centre, could be developed so as to take some jobs from central London; thus the precise effects on commuting patterns, now fiercely debated, could and should be quantified. Or there could be more scatter of jobs in the suburbs, to bring the possibility of part-time work to many married women now locked in their homes. Though a higher proportion of married women work in London than in the country as a whole, the process need not have reached its limits. If labour is to continue scarce in London, and there is no evidence otherwise, it will be essential to test various ways of using more of it.

One particularly attractive policy would be for London to build what an American planner has called New Towns Intown. Like any other new towns, these would have town centres, located at nodal points for transport, where many different routes of different types converged: the radial main railway lines running in towards the main line termini, the existing and the planned new tube lines, the suburban bus routes converging on railway stations, the new ring motorways (assuming that at least some of them are built). In the future London, these will be the points where people change one form of transport for another: the incoming car commuter would leave his car and take a train on into central London, the housewife visiting a friend would change from the train to an express motorway bus. At the same time, like many of our newest new towns, these sites would be towns already: they would have shops and some offices, possibly ripe for renewal and redevelopment. Ealing in the west, Ilford in the east, Croydon in the south are examples.

At such points, the plan would encourage new concentrations of jobs. Since factory employment in London is declining anyway, and factories do not locate in city centres, the new jobs would be in offices, shops, restaurants and pubs and hotels, television and radio studios, polytechnics. Thus the New Towns Intown would be major shopping and entertainment centres, offering the same facilities as a large provincial town like Leicester or Newcastle. This is not fanciful: in fact it is already true of Croydon, one possible illustrative model of the London of the future.

Notice that this does not assume, necessarily, any increase in the total number of jobs in London.

These alternatives hinge in part on the total amount of jobs in London. Of course, in large measure that is a quantity within the control of the planning system. By manipulating incentives and disincentives, financial and physical controls, the planning machine as a whole – including relevant central Government departments – could achieve a greater increase in Greater London employment or an equally greater decline. What is lacking is a rationale for either course of action. The GLC have argued, without convincing anyone so far, that productivity in London manufacturing industries is greater than in the same industries elsewhere. They could hardly even try to make the same argument for service industry; the evidence is completely lacking. All that is well known is some of the social cost of London employment in terms of housing and transport subsidy. Like it or not, people are voting against life in London with their feet. The upshot is that to staff even a static total of jobs, let alone a rising one, London's public authorities will be forced either to build more heavily subsidized housing near to the work, or further subsidize commuter services, or both. These subsidies will be paid for, either by the general taxpayer in Lancashire or in Wester Ross (if he can be persuaded), or by the general ratepayer in London, whether he be in secure employment and unsubsidized housing, or an old-age pensioner. So, with regard to jobs, London finds itself on the horns of a truly desperate dilemma.

The employment problem is thus linked inexorably to the housing problem, is indeed its origin. A brutal fact is that a large proportion of the total population of London cannot afford the capital cost of ownership, and perhaps never will be able to do so unaided. Since this majority occupies some of the most expensive land in Britain, either it must accept lower space standards than

the average, or take massive subsidies from the rest of the population, or both. In a laissez faire situation, supposing the labour
supply to be reasonably tight, workers would manage to pass on
some of their extra housing costs to employers, forcing them
either to pass some of the extra wage cost on to customers, or to
economize on labour, or both. Thus either service levels in central
London hotels would decline, with a bigger emphasis on self-
service (as in America or Sweden), or hotel bills would rise
sharply (as, again, in the high-wage economies of the United
States or Scandinavia). At present neither happens. Thus one can
witness the supreme paradox of foreign visitors extolling London
as a cheap city, while massive subsidies are needed to support
public housing programmes for service workers on expensive
land. If the balance of payments crisis were that acute, this might
be justified as an emergency measure; the trouble is that this
situation existed long before anyone thought of that particular
feeble justification.

Subsidy programmes, however misguided and distorted, cannot be dismantled overnight. There are existing commitments
made honourably, there are wider moral commitments not to
heap sudden burdens on unsuspecting sections of the population.
But that does not provide an excuse for prevarication; indeed the
reverse. London planners at least ought to follow through the
logical implications of possible, even unlikely, changes in central
Government policy: for instance, withdrawing the high density
and expensive land subsidies, or substituting a total system of
subsidy based on income for the present illogical system based
on tenure, or encouraging the poor to move from congested
locations to more spacious new and expanded town sites. Radical
changes in the subsidy system are promised, which makes this
even more urgent. The removal of the subsidy on British Rail
commuter lines has profound implications for the future structure of the housing market in London. So indeed will any changes
in transport finance, whether in the public sector or affecting the
use of the private car. So they should look at the wisdom or otherwise of the whole present structure of transport subsidy and
taxation. There is, to put it mildly, something anomalous about

a system which subsidizes the very rich for buying expensive houses on mortgage and then subsidizes them again by building motorways to drive their cars on (supported by the preposterous old LCC policy of providing office garage space free of charge for company directors), while the very poor in privately rented housing get no subsidy at all.

At least, London planners should look at the following policy alternatives for jobs and homes and transport. In each case, to try to be impartial, I shall state the reverse of the policy which most obviously occurs. Most of the policy choices, it will doubtless be noted, are for central government; as things now stand, they are quite outside the control of the GLC.

1) End all differential subsidies on expensive sites, or for high-rise construction. (*Alternative: increase the differential.*) Instead, introduce a system that aids the poorest most, whatever their form of tenure; modify this if desired by some additional allowance for inner London (on a 'fair rent' basis), but massively increase the information services about available housing in new and expanding towns outside London. This last would include specialized housing counsellors available in each district to ease people's movement from London.

2) Introduce a payroll tax on employment in congested areas, coupled with a scheme of incentive payments for each employee in development areas (with a neutral zone in between, probably including the outer metropolitan area); scrap all other incentive and control systems, including Industrial Development Certificates and Office Development Permits licensing schemes; thus, in future, employers may locate where they wish, so long as they pay the price. (*Alternative: do nothing.*)

3) Subsidize long-distance commuting by public transport by aid to the railways; use this partly to improve the level of off-peak services, thus making it easier for service workers on irregular hours to commute. (For instance, one commuter service might run at regular intervals all night. The new city of Milton Keynes might be an ideal opportunity for such an experiment, since the available rail service is very good, and this line must be kept in operation all night for freight.) This might be coupled with the

information service under (1), to encourage low-paid shift workers to move to a new town. Eventually, the object would be to incorporate these workers within the labour force of the new city. (*Alternative: cut out any form of transport subsidy, direct or indirect.*)

4) Allow London to develop beyond the Green Belt, either by a straight expansion of the administrative area to take in the belt within abouty twenty-five miles of the centre (Slough, Watford, Hatfield, Harlow, Tilbury, Dartford, Reigate, Gatwick, Weybridge, Woking), or by allowing London to incorporate discontinuous areas of new development, for instance all or part of the new growth areas proposed in the 1970 *Strategic Plan for the South East.* This would help solve, or would solve completely, the rateable value dilemma which London is experiencing and which it may experience more seriously in the future. (*Alternative: do nothing, just as now.*)

5) Bring down the cost of new owner-occupied housing built on formerly undeveloped land in the outer metropolitan area, by a development corporation mechanism similar to that in new towns. Such a corporation would buy the land needed for development in the new major growth areas suggested in the 1970 plan on the same terms as new town corporations, i.e. at agricultural value plus certain allowances. It could be sold on long lease to private or public developments. Speculators' profit, the inevitable result of planning permission under present conditions, would be eliminated. This, coupled with other measures, could aid the move of a wider cross-section of the population from London, rather than trying to rehouse such people on expensive land within the metropolis itself. (*Alternative: go on paying differential subsidy.*)

6) Develop the major strategic or sectoral centres to take a much more rapid increase of a wider range of activities, coupled with operation of disincentives to operation in central London, so as to effect an internal redistribution of London's jobs. Possibly, redevelop the zones immediately around these centres to a higher residential density than now, to reduce the burden of journeys to new centres. (*Alternative: do nothing, but let central London rip.*)

Each of these policies would have certain implications for transport planning. At present, transport alternatives in London tend to be presented in crude, oversimplified either-or terms, as a road versus public transport conflict. In fact the debate is wider than that. One critical question is how much transport investment of all sorts London should have in relation to the rest of the country. It is all very well arguing that Ringway 1 does not justify its cost of construction; the Fleet line and then the Wimbledon line may not either, for at present it is simply not known. Related to this, and to the whole question of activity patterns, is where the investment emphasis should lie within London. For instance, it is clear that the inner ringways have much higher costs than the outer ones, but also much higher benefits; the precise relationships between benefits and costs are open to debate. If the emphasis were on development in the outer metropolitan area, investment in the orbital motorway round London (and mainly outside the GLC area) would show a better return. If the emphasis were on the sector centres, then Ringway 2 (which passes near most of them) would look better. If there were greater emphasis on the centre (and perhaps only if) large scale extensions of the underground system would appear justified.

The need to choose

Thus, we need not one vision of a future London, but several, all with their consequences spelt out and costed, in so far as that is possible. But visions are an essential part of the planning process. At some point the whole careful process of survey, of projection, of considering parameters and constraints, must gel into an actual design. The great advance in plan-making during the last ten years has been the emphasis on creating and then evaluating alternative design patterns. It is this, above all, that is lacking from the plan now under scrutiny in the inquiry.

Which of the visions is preferable? Probably none considered in isolation. Different strategies need to be used to complement and support each other. But their broad drift should be clear. Londoners, and their government, are now faced with an impossible set of contradictions, which need to be resolved. Employment, both in the centre and in the inner ring, needs to be reduced to the level which can be manned by a diminishing work force. That work force needs to fall to the level where it can be housed without special subsidies for expensive forms of construction; and there should be a massive campaign to remove London's poorer families to decent environments outside. The fall in jobs and in labour force will be sharply selective, taking out of London those activities which have least need to be there; much of this will be self-selection through the operation of incentives and disincentives, but there may have to be major decisions to move parts of the public sector such as Government agencies or universities. The pattern of employment also probably needs redistributing internally, with less in the centre and more in the sectoral centres of the suburbs.

There will be financial implications for London government, which may need to be resolved by giving London new rateable value outside its present boundaries. But alternatively, London could be given new sources of revenue, to be paid for by the many people who are not residents but make use of its services. A sales tax would tap the many visitors from the rest of the country or abroad, who throng the Oxford Street shops; a hotels tax would directly take revenue from the overseas visitor. No one should underestimate the need here. For at present, increasingly, London government is being driven to adopt perverse policies, policies bad for it people and for the country as a whole, through threat of penury.

Notes on the Contributors

DAVID WILCOX. Planning correspondent of the *Evening Standard*

DEREK SENIOR. Member of the Royal Commission on local government, former local government and planning correspondent of the *Guardian*

JANE MORTON. Housing correspondent of *New Society*

PROFESSOR PETER COWAN. Head of Planning Studies, University College, London

JOHN BLAKE. Planner with one of the London boroughs

J. M. THOMSON. Rees-Jeffreys research fellow in transport economics, London School of Economics

TERENCE BENDIXSON. Journalist. Former planning correspondent of the *Guardian*

STEPHEN MULLIN. Architect in private practice and regular contributor to the *New Statesman*

SAM WEBB. Architect with one of the London boroughs

SYLVIA WEBB. Architect working as a partner in Fairweather and Webb

PROFESSOR PETER HALL. Head of geography department, Reading University, member South-East Economic Planning Council

Bibliography

Greater London Development Plan Statement, GLC, 1969

Greater London Development Plan Report of Studies, GLC, 1969

Movement in London, GLC, 1969

Tomorrow's London, GLC, 1969

North East London – Some Implications of the Greater London Development Plan, Colin Buchanan and Partners, GLC, 1969

Housing in Camden, Ruth Glass, Centre for Urban Studies, 1968

London's Housing Needs, Ruth Glass and John Westergaard, CUS, 1965

The South East Study, HMSO, 1964

The Strategy for the South East, HMSO, 1967

Strategic Plan for the South East, HMSO, 1970

London Under Stress, Town and Country Planning Association 105, 1970

More About Penguins

Penguinews, which appears every month, contains
details of all the new books issued by Penguins
as they are published. From time to time it is
supplemented by *Penguins in Print*, which is a
complete list of all books published by Penguins
which are in print. (There are well over three
thousand of these.)

A specimen copy of *Penguinews* will be sent to
you free on request, and you can become a
subscriber for the price of the postage. For a
year's issues (including the complete lists) please
send 25p if you live in the United Kingdom, or
50p if you live elsewhere. Just write to Dept EP,
Penguin Books Ltd, Harmondsworth, Middlesex,
enclosing a cheque or postal order, and your
name will be added to the mailing list.

Some other books published by Penguins are
described on the following pages.

Note : *Penguinews* and *Penguins in Print* are not
available in the U.S.A. or Canada

a Penguin Special

Traffic in Towns

The specially shortened edition of the Buchanan Report

'We are nourishing a monster of great potential
destructiveness.'

The motor car is the menace that prompted Professor Colin
Buchanan's famous report, *Traffic in Towns*. This is the
most comprehensive, objective, and radical examination
of urban traffic and its effect on the conditions of urban
living that has ever been made.

Because of its profuse illustrations the H.M.S.O. edition
of *Traffic in Towns* had necessarily to be published at
£2·50. This Penguin edition is a condensation which has
been approved by Professor Buchanan and which omits
none of the main arguments or conclusions of the report.
It permits this important document to appear at a price
at which a very much wider public can comprehend the
gigantic and terrifyingly urgent task with which Britain
is now faced.

a Pelican Original

Man and Environment

Crisis and the Strategy of Choice

Robert Arvill

What will the world look and be like tomorrow? Must
the landscape be an extension of today's spreading
deterioration? More air fouled by noise and poisoned
fumes; more water polluted by chemicals and oil slicks;
more land crushed under the sprawl of towns,
super-highways, airports, factories, pylons, and
strip-mines? Is man bound to build a stifling
steel-and-concrete hell for himself? Or can effective
steps be taken now to preserve our open-spaces, seashores,
and life-sustaining elements from the assaults of
technology?

This is a book about man – about the devastating impact
of his numbers on the environment and the decisions and
actions he can take to attack the problem. The author is
an expert on conservation and planning. Land, air, water,
and wildlife are treated by him as both valuable resources
in very short supply and as precious living entities. He
contrasts present management of these resources with
man's future needs. British experience and examples from
all over the world illustrate the critical and practical aspects
of the problem. Past conservation programmes are reviewed
and evaluated and the book offers a complete set of
proposals for regional, national, and international action
on environmental protection. The approach is farsighted,
informed, urgent.

a Penguin Special

Paying For Roads

The Economics of Traffic Congestion

G. J. Roth

If we are to avoid traffic-thrombosis in large towns we must adopt a completely new approach to road provision and traffic congestion. Economics can provide such an approach.

Electricity and gas, food and clothing, are distributed in accordance with what the customer is prepared to pay. Is there any reason, apart from the sentimental aura which surrounds 'The Queen's Highway', why we shouldn't provide city roads in accordance with what the users are prepared to pay?

Paying for Roads has been specially written for the layman by a transport economist to explain the pricing and investment principles that could usefully be applied to the commodity 'road space'.

The criterion of profitability may be foreign to many planners nowadays; but its application to city roads could reduce congestion and simultaneously direct to road improvement all the funds that motorists would *choose* to provide.

a Pelican Original

Noise

Rupert Taylor

To understand what noise is and what can be done about it needs – at the very least – a knowledge of acoustics, economics, law, mathematics, physics, and physiology. By skilful exposition Rupert Taylor has made the contribution of each discipline perfectly clear to the interested layman, whether he manages a foundry, wishes to build a silent motor-cycle, or merely lives beneath Concorde's projected flight-path.

Mr Taylor's plentiful diagrams and tables elaborate a lively and well-ordered text, enabling his readers to decide for themselves whether a reduction of ten decibels is worth having—or even meaningful; whether the bedroom wall will transmit noise, reflect it, or turn it into heat; what risks of permanent hearing damage they are already running; or how to encourage an impedance mis-match.

a Pelican Original

Los Angeles

Reyner Banham

Los Angeles, though often dismissed as some kind of environmental disaster, is also admitted to have had a more creative record in architecture in the present century than any other American city except, perhaps, Chicago.

It is, above all, ignorance of the true nature of the Los Angeles environment that produces this paradox of views, and in this pioneering study of the city as an ecology for architecture, Reyner Banham sets the works of designers as diverse as Frank Lloyd Wright, Charles Eames, Richard Neutra, or Simon Rodia (who designed the famous Watts towers) in their proper landscape of mountains, plains, beaches, and freeways, and shows the complex interplay of powers and concepts – from Spanish ranches to the Environmental Goals Programme – that have shaped both the architecture and the human ecology that enshrines it.

a Pelican Original

Participating in Local Affairs

Dilys M. Hill

To most people, local politics are much more remote than
national affairs. Local councils often seem to be merely
bureaucratic branches of Whitehall, and the men who
prime the parish pump are seen as time-servers, Gradgrinds,
or at best dull provincial worthies. Yet if ever democracy
works, it should do so at the local level. What is wrong
with our local government, and how can people involve
themselves in the decisions which shape their lives?

Dilys Hill, who discussed the issues of participation with
the Maud and Skeffington Committees, has written a serious
survey of the problems of individuals and groups in relation
to local government. Knowing that 'participation' and
'involvement' can easily become colour-supplement
catch-phrases, she gives very concrete answers to three
fundamental questions: Who really makes the decisions in
local government? How can people become active in local
affairs? And what reforms in the structure of local
administration would improve the quality of communal life?